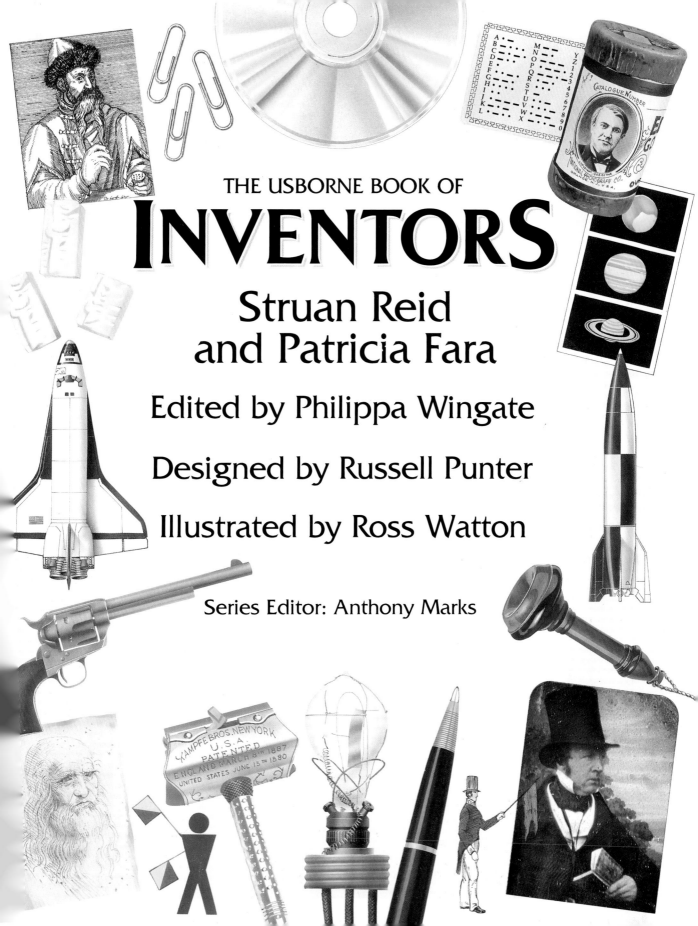

THE USBORNE BOOK OF

INVENTORS

Struan Reid
and Patricia Fara

Edited by Philippa Wingate

Designed by Russell Punter

Illustrated by Ross Watton

Series Editor: Anthony Marks

Contents

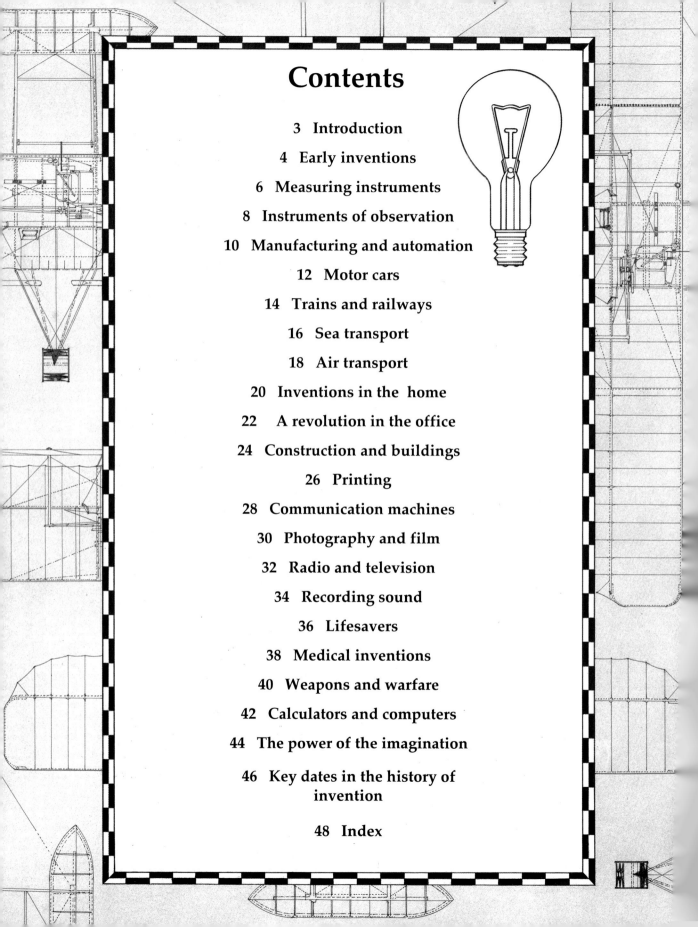

Introduction

Inventors and inventions

An inventor is someone who discovers or produces a useful object or process that did not exist before. This book is about the lives and work of the people who invented many of the things we take for granted today.

Many inventions enable people to do things they could not do before; others help them to work more efficiently. Some inventions, like the telephone or television, have had a dramatic effect on the way people live. But while others may seem less revolutionary, they have had equally important consequences. For example, the invention of the harness for horses changed the course of history, because it allowed people to use horses for long journeys and to pull heavy loads.

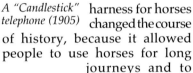

A "Candlestick" telephone (1905)

Modern invention

Modern inventions are rarely the product of a single inventor's efforts. For example, no single individual can claim that he or she alone invented the silicon chip. Thousands of people have played a useful role in its development and manufacture, and many thousands more have improved its design.

A silicon chip

Many companies employ teams of people to work on new ideas. For example, the managing director of the Japanese company Sony wanted a device which would allow him to listen to music while he played golf. As a result, a team of company technicians developed the Sony Walkman, the first personal stereo.

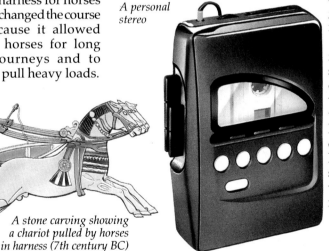

A personal stereo

Continuous invention

Many inventions have taken several centuries to develop into their modern forms, so it is impossible to give a precise date for their creation. The history of the invention of the piano, for example, lasts more than 2,000 years. Experts have calculated that more than 2,000 separate inventions and developments have contributed to the construction of modern pianos.

A dulcimer, one of the forerunners of the piano, shown in a 16th-century tapestry

Patenting inventions

When an inventor produces a new device, he or she usually applies for a patent. This is a document which gives the inventor the exclusive right to make and sell the invention.

Some people died rich and famous having made a fortune from selling their inventions, others died in poverty, unrecognized for their achievements. In this book, you can read about the lives of both the successful and the unsuccessful inventors.

Whitcomb Judson's 1893 patent for the zip fastener

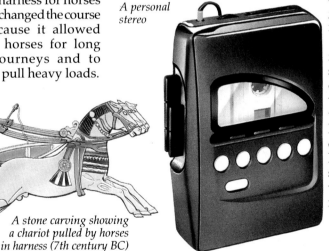

A stone carving showing a chariot pulled by horses in harness (7th century BC)

Dates

Some of the dates in this book are from the period before the birth of Christ. They are indicated by the letters BC. Early dates in the period after Christ's birth are indicated by the letters AD. Some dates are preceded by the abbreviation *c*, which stands for "circa", the Latin for "about". It is used by historians to show they are unsure exactly when a particular event took place.

About this book

Each section in this book is a history of inventors and inventions in a particular field, such as medicine, communications and transport. On pages 46-47 a chart outlines the main developments described in the book.

Beside the title of every chapter, you will find a small picture or cartoon relating to an invention on those pages. You could try guessing what they are. There is a list of the answers on page 48.

Early inventions

As soon as the first people appeared on the Earth, about half a million years ago, they started to use materials like stone and wood to make their lives more comfortable. These people were the first inventors.

It is difficult to find information about early inventors. We can often only guess at how early people accomplished many of the things they did. For example, we are still unsure exactly how the Ancient Egyptians built their pyramids so accurately.

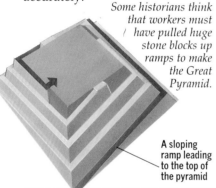

Some historians think that workers must have pulled huge stone blocks up ramps to make the Great Pyramid.

A sloping ramp leading to the top of the pyramid

Isolated inventions

Before roads and ocean-going ships were built, many communities were isolated. Individual inventors devised their own solutions to common problems, such as how to build solid houses, kill animals or prepare food.

Certain solutions appeared independently in different places around the world, like China, South America and Egypt. But some inventions used by one group of people simply did not exist anywhere else. For centuries the use of gunpowder and the manufacture of silk were only known in China. Inventions only became more universal when people began to travel, trading goods and exchanging ideas.

Early building

The earliest stone buildings were constructed with flat roofs supported by stone beams on upright posts. Roman builders, using new inventions like arches and concrete, were able to build larger, stronger buildings like the one shown here. Many of these buildings still survive today.

Building a Roman villa

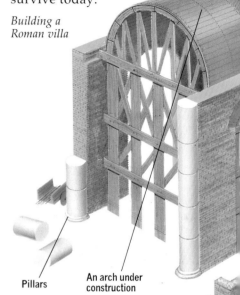

Pillars

An arch under construction

The wheel

No one knows exactly when or where the wheel first appeared. Most scholars believe that it was first used by potters in about 3500BC, either in Mesopotamia (modern Iraq) or in the central or eastern parts of Europe. The first known transport wheel appears in a Mesopotamian picture dated to c.3200BC. The picture shows a cart with solid wheels held together by metal brackets.

Wheeled transport was not used in America before the arrival of European explorers at the end of the 15th century. This may have been because there was a lack of suitable domesticated animals for pulling carts.

The development of the wheel

Mosaic of 3200BC showing wheels held together by brackets

| Wheel in three sections, fixed by brackets | Lighter spoked wheel from Egypt, 1500BC | Greek eight-spoked wheel, c.400BC | A Roman wheel of c.AD100 | Wheel designed by Leonardo da Vinci, late 15th century | An early motor car wheel |

The arch

An arch is made of wedge-shaped stones, held together by pressure. Arches which date from c.3000BC have been found at Ur, in Iraq. The Assyrians and Babylonians also used arches. The 6th-century Ishtar Gate of Babylon is made of sun-dried bricks. The Romans used arches to construct tall buildings like amphitheatres or aqueducts.

Constructing an arch

A wooden frame in the shape of an arch was constructed between stone columns.

Wedge-shaped stones were then built on the frame. The weight of the stones held them in place.

Arches were very heavy, so supports called buttresses were used to take the strain.

Strong walls were formed from two brick walls filled with concrete.

Once the concrete had dried, another wall could be built on top in the same way.

Tiles and gutters of baked clay were stamped with the name of the factory at which they were produced.

Central heating

The Romans were masters of home comforts and devised a central heating system in the 1st century AD. It was called the hypocaust and was mainly used to heat public baths, but in cold climates it was also used to heat houses. This Roman invention was forgotten in the West when the Roman Empire collapsed in the 5th century.

A Roman hypocaust

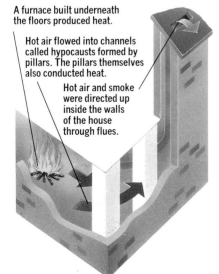

A furnace built underneath the floors produced heat.

Hot air flowed into channels called hypocausts formed by pillars. The pillars themselves also conducted heat.

Hot air and smoke were directed up inside the walls of the house through flues.

Writing

In about 3200BC, the Sumerians of Mesopotamia were the first people to write. Their script used pictures to represent words and is known as "pictographic writing".

Some early pictographic symbols and their meanings.

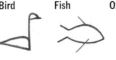

Bird   Fish   Ox   Grain   To stand or go

A stone tablet carved with pictographic writing (c.3000BC)

Five hundred years later, nearby people, like the Babylonians, Persians and Assyrians, had adapted this kind of writing into a type known as cuneiform (meaning "wedge-shaped"). They used a reed with a triangular-shaped end to make inscriptions in clay.

How to make clay tablets with cuneiform inscriptions

The cuneiform symbols for ox and grain

  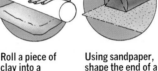

Roll a piece of clay into a pancake and then cut it into small squares.

Using sandpaper, shape the end of a stick into a triangular point.

Press the reed into the surface of the clay to form the symbols.

Ox

Grain

By about 1300BC, at Ugarit in Syria, the first alphabet had evolved from cuneiform. It contained 32 letters, each representing a single sound, which could be joined together to form a word. The Greeks adopted this system, which is the ancestor of the European alphabet.

In Egypt, in 3000BC, a writing system known as hieroglyphs was introduced. This used symbols to represent words, sounds or letters.

These Egyptian hieroglyphs spell out the name of the Egyptian queen Cleopatra

C   L   E   O   P   A   T   R   A

Money

Throughout history, many different things have been used for barter and exchange, such as copper bars, precious stones, shells and cattle. But as trade between nations increased, a standard, easy form of exchange was needed. The invention of money enabled deals to be carried out quickly using coins of an agreed value.

The first proper coinage was introduced in 700BC by King Gyges of Lydia (now in Turkey). The Lydian coins were made of a metal called electrum (a natural mixture of gold and silver) and were stamped with the king's emblem.

The king's emblem was a lion and a bull.

A mark was imprinted on the coin.

Two sides of a coin issued in about 550BC by King Croesus of Lydia

Measuring instruments

People have always attempted to measure quantities such as length, weight and time. Countless inventors, many of them now unknown or forgotten, have gradually improved the design of measuring instruments. Today, there are even devices that can measure things which are not visible to the naked eye, such as subatomic particles.

Early clocks

Sundials were the first method of charting the passing of time. In ancient times, water clocks and candles were employed, but they were never very accurate.

A 13th-century water clock, built for an Arab sultan

Every half hour this bird whistled.

This man made the falcon beside him release a pellet into the dragon's mouth.

The dragon began to wriggle. The pellet hit a gong inside the elephant before it fell into a bowl.

The elephant driver beats a rhythm every half hour

A new way of measuring time

The first mechanical clock, driven by weights, was made by Gerbert, a French monk who in 999 became Pope Sylvester II. Many further changes were introduced until, in 1300, fairly accurate mechanical clocks were used in Europe. A device called a verge escapement turned the hands.

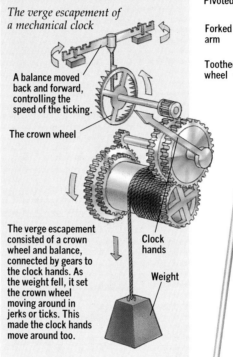

The verge escapement of a mechanical clock

A balance moved back and forward, controlling the speed of the ticking.

The crown wheel

The verge escapement consisted of a crown wheel and balance, connected by gears to the clock hands. As the weight fell, it set the crown wheel moving around in jerks or ticks. This made the clock hands move around too.

Clock hands

Weight

Pendulums

In 1656, Christian Huygens (1629-95), a Dutch physicist, invented the first accurate pendulum clock. Its design was based on an idea suggested by Galileo Galilei (1564-1642; see page 8). Galileo had observed that pendulums always swing back and forward at regular intervals. Huygens developed a way of keeping a pendulum swinging while linking its movement to the hands of a clock dial through a series of toothed wheels.

A reconstruction of Galileo's pendulum escapement

Pivoted lever

Forked arm

Toothed wheel

Cog wheels

The swing of the pendulum made the pivoted lever and the forked arm turn the toothed wheel.

The movement of the toothed wheel turned the cog wheels.

The pendulum always took an identical period of time to swing backward and forward.

A new kind of map

A map is a two-dimensional representation of the Earth's surface. But the Earth is spherical, which means that the shapes on early maps are distorted. In 1569, Gerardus Mercator (1512-94), a Flemish geographer and map-maker, introduced a more accurate way of drawing maps than had previously been used. He drew the world as though it was a cylinder divided up by parallel horizontal and vertical lines, called lines of latitude and longitude. In 1585, Mercator published an atlas of maps drawn using his new system. His method is still used in atlases today.

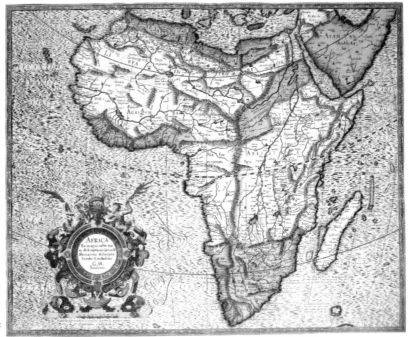

A map of Africa from Mercator's Atlas

Under pressure

Evangelista Torricelli (1608-47), was the son of an Italian textile worker. He experimented with vacuums and pressure. In 1643, he produced a device, now known as a mercury barometer, which is used to measure atmospheric pressure.

How Torricelli's barometer worked

A bowl was half-filled with mercury. The open end of a test tube full of mercury was placed under the surface of the mercury in the bowl.

Some of the mercury in the tube ran out into the bowl. As a result the level of the mercury in the tube fell.

The height of the column of mercury in the tube was directly affected by the magnitude of atmospheric pressure. It could, therefore, be used to measure atmospheric pressure.

Torricelli and his barometer

Measuring temperature

For thousands of years, people measured temperature by noting the expansion of a liquid as it is heated. But by the 17th century there were over 30 scales of measurement, so comparing readings from different thermometers was difficult. In 1742, Anders Celsius (1701-44), a Swedish astronomer devised a standard scale for the measurement of temperature. It is called the Celsius scale and contains a hundred degrees. Each degree is one hundredth of the temperature difference between the boiling and freezing points of water.

One of the first thermometers to use the Celsius scale

Absolute zero

Jacques Charles (1746-1823), a French physicist noticed that when a gas cooled, its volume contracted by 1/273 for every fall of one degree Celsius in its temperature. William Thomson (1824-1907), another physicist, suggested that at –273°C, the energy of motion of gas molecules must have reached zero. Thomson, who was awarded the title Baron Kelvin of Largs for his achievements, devised a new temperature scale in which 0°K (which is called absolute zero) is the equivalent of –273°C. Known today as the Kelvin scale, it helps scientists measure very low temperatures.

Detecting radiation

In 1908, German-born physicist Hans Geiger (1882-1945), invented a hand-held machine used to detect radiation in the air. It is now called the Geiger counter. When radiation is present, the machine makes a clicking noise. The level of radiation is counted and shown on a dial.

An early Geiger counter

Low pressure gas in a copper cylinder

Wire inside the counter

When radioactive particles entered the tube, an electric pulse passed between the wire and the cylinder's walls. The pulses were detected by a counter.

Instruments of observation

People have always wanted to see things more closely than is possible with the naked eye. The first magnifying lenses were made about 700BC in the Middle East. Since that time, developments have helped people to see the world in greater detail. Today, the electron microscope can even make the invisible visible.

An astronomical lens

One of the first people to make a practical telescope was Hans Lippershey (c.1570-1619), a Dutch optician. It consisted of a long tube with a magnifying lens at each end. The combined effect of two lenses enabled him to see distant objects in greater detail than with the naked eye.

A controversial view

Galileo Galilei (1564-1642), born in Pisa, Italy, studied medicine and became a university lecturer. In 1592, he built a telescope which magnified objects about 30 times. He used it to examine the Moon and the movement of the planets.

Galileo using his telescope

In 1632, Galileo wrote *Dialogue Concerning the Two Chief World Systems*. He supported the views of Copernicus, a Polish monk, who claimed that the Earth revolved around the Sun. This idea clashed with the teachings of the Roman Catholic Church, which said that the planets revolved around the Earth. Galileo was convicted for holding a view contrary to the teachings of the Church.

Eyepiece

Galileo's telescope of c.1609

Reflecting telescopes

In 1668, an English scientist named Isaac Newton (1642-1727) built a new kind of telescope, using mirrors as well as lenses to direct the rays of light from an object onto the observer's eye. This reduced the blurring which had previously been caused by imperfections in the lenses. This is known as a reflecting telescope.

Newton's design was improved by William Herschel (1738-1822), a German astronomer, who studied astronomy in England. He incorporated giant mirrors with diameters of 1.2m (4ft), which collected more light and enabled him to see very distant objects. With this powerful new telescope, Herschel and his sister Caroline (1750-1848) studied the skies. They discovered the planet Uranus and many new stars and comets.

Newton's reflecting telescope (1668)

Herschel's giant reflecting telescope

Light rays from the object were collected by a mirror at the base of the telescope.

Eyepiece

This mirror directed the light to the eyepiece

The telescope was mounted on a wooden ball so that it could be swivelled.

Telescope tube made of iron

The observer stood at the top of the telescope and communicated observations to an assistant in a hut at the base through a speaking tube.

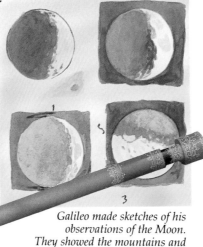

Galileo made sketches of his observations of the Moon. They showed the mountains and "seas" that he had seen.

Examining small objects

The first microscope was probably invented by Hans Janssen, a Dutchman, at the end of the 16th century. It contained one lens that produced a magnified image of an object, and a second lens that enlarged the magnified image.

A prolific inventor of scientific instruments, the Englishman Robert Hooke (1635-1703), built an instrument that produced clearer images than Janssen's device. In 1665, Hooke published a book called the *Micrographia*, which contained beautiful engraved plates of his drawings of objects seen through his microscope.

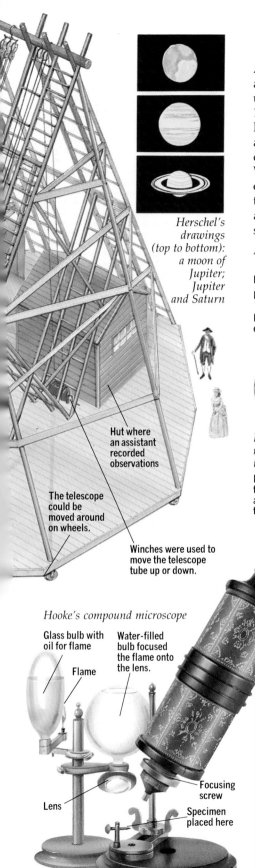

Herschel's drawings (top to bottom): a moon of Jupiter; Jupiter and Saturn

Hut where an assistant recorded observations

The telescope could be moved around on wheels.

Winches were used to move the telescope tube up or down.

The electron microscope

All matter is made of atoms which are so tiny that they cannot be seen under ordinary microscopes. In 1933, two German scientists, Max Kroll and Ernst Ruska, developed an electron microscope which could produce an image of an atom. When tiny particles of atoms, called electrons, are fired at a specimen, it too emits electrons. These produce a three-dimensional image of the specimen on a screen.

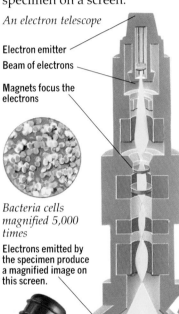

An electron telescope

Electron emitter

Beam of electrons

Magnets focus the electrons

Bacteria cells magnified 5,000 times

Electrons emitted by the specimen produce a magnified image on this screen.

Eyepiece

Radar

Robert Watson-Watt (1892-1973), a Scottish physicist, first developed a system called radar (Radio Detecting and Ranging). The system sends out radio waves, and any object they meet reflects them back. The pattern of reflections indicates how far away the object is, its speed and direction.

Watson-Watt first used radio waves to detect storms which were endangering aircraft. In 1935, he built a long-range radar system which could detect aircraft up to 64km (40 miles) away. The system was vital in helping Britain to defend itself from air attack during World War II.

A radar image of a hurricane near Mexico

A radar station built on the British coast during World War II

Hooke's compound microscope

Glass bulb with oil for flame

Water-filled bulb focused the flame onto the lens.

Flame

Focusing screw

Lens

Specimen placed here

Spectacles and contact lenses

In 1280, an Italian physicist named Salvino degli Armati (1245-1317) is thought to have made the first pair of glasses. These contained two convex lenses, which magnified objects so that people could see them more easily.

Leonardo da Vinci (see page 45) experimented with the idea of contact lenses. In *Codex on the Eye*, he described a water-filled tube sealed with a lens which could correct eye defects. Da Vinci's idea was tested in the 18th century by Thomas Young and John Herschel (son of William Herschel). A layer of transparent gel was put on Herschel's eye to correct his eye defect.

Contact lenses made in about 1930

An illustration of hand-held spectacles (1493)

Manufacturing and automation

By the end of the 18th century, more people were starting to work in huge factories, manufacturing a variety of goods. The introduction of new inventions led to great increases in the production of cloth, iron, pottery and coal. This period of rapid technological change is called the Industrial Revolution.

Increasing output

Cloth making was the first manufacturing process to be greatly altered by new inventions. In 1733, John Kay (1704-c.1764), an English weaver, mechanized weaving when he invented the "flying shuttle". It doubled the amount of cloth a person could produce in one day.

In 1764, another English weaver named James Hargreaves (c.1722-78) invented the Spinning Jenny.

The Spinning Jenny

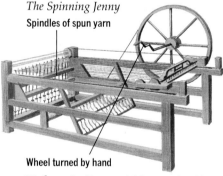

Spindles of spun yarn

Wheel turned by hand

Eight spindles could be worked by a hand-turned wheel, so a single operator could spin eight threads. In 1771, Richard Arkwright (1732-92) built a water-powered spinning machine that produced stronger thread than the Spinning Jenny.

Arkwright's spinning machine

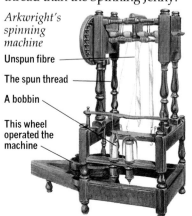

Unspun fibre

The spun thread

A bobbin

This wheel operated the machine

A steam-driven toy

The use of steam as a source of power can be traced back as far as the 1st century AD, to a Greek engineer named Hero of Alexandria. He designed a toy consisting of a metal sphere filled with water. The sphere was heated over a fire. When the water inside it boiled, steam began to escape from two holes on opposite sides of the sphere. This produced a force that caused the sphere to rotate.

Hero considered his invention no more than a clever toy.

Steam engines

In the 18th century, giant steam engines were used to power machinery. The first was made in 1698, by Thomas Savery (c.1650-1715), an English engineer. Inside the engine, steam from a boiler passed into the cylinder. A plunger, called a piston, was forced out of the cylinder by the pressure of the steam. Cold water was sprayed onto the cylinder to cool and condense the steam. This produced a much lower pressure inside the cylinder, causing the piston to fall again. His engine was used to pump water out of flooded mines.

Later, Thomas Newcomen (1663-1729), another Englishman, improved Savery's machine, which often broke down. In Newcomen's machine the piston was chained to one end of a wooden crossbeam. The pumping machinery was attached to the other end.

Newcomen's steam engine

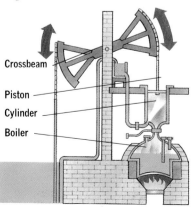

Crossbeam

Piston

Cylinder

Boiler

In 1777, an engineer named James Watt (1736-1819) designed an engine with a separate condenser, into which steam from the cylinder was passed and cooled. This allowed the engine to be kept hot, reducing fuel consumption and saving time.

Watt's steam engine became the main source of power in Britain's textile mills.

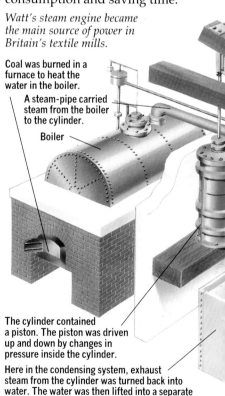

Coal was burned in a furnace to heat the water in the boiler.

A steam-pipe carried steam from the boiler to the cylinder.

Boiler

The cylinder contained a piston. The piston was driven up and down by changes in pressure inside the cylinder.

Here in the condensing system, exhaust steam from the cylinder was turned back into water. The water was then lifted into a separate tank, and pumped back to the boiler.

Exhaust steam

Water

Tank

Water pumped into the boiler

Sewing machines

The first sewing machine was designed in 1830, by a French tailor named Barthélemy Thimonnier. A wheel, powered by a foot pedal, raised and lowered a needle. It could sew 200 stitches in a minute, compared to the 30 stitches of a tailor. But many tailors feared they would lose their jobs, and an angry mob destroyed 80 of the machines.

Elias Howe (1819-67), an American engineer, also developed a sewing machine. But to support his family he was forced to sell his invention for a small sum of money. Later he found that Isaac Singer (1811-76) was selling sewing machines based on his original design. In 1854, Howe launched a law case against Singer, in which he won the right to receive payment for all sewing machines sold in the USA.

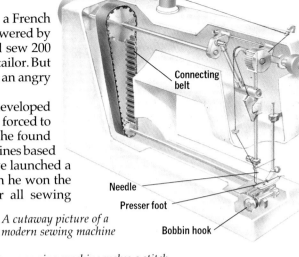

Needle thread

Connecting belt

Needle

Presser foot

Bobbin hook

A cutaway picture of a modern sewing machine

Thimonnier using his sewing machine, patented in 1830

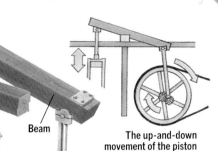

An early sewing machine

Needle

How a sewing machine makes a stitch

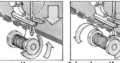

The needle pierces the cloth.

A hook on the bobbin catches the needle thread.

The needle thread is looped around the bobbin.

The needle rises and pulls the stitch tight.

Robots

A robot is a machine that can be instructed to perform tasks. One of the first robotic devices was the automatic pilot, invented in 1913, by an American named Elmer Sperry (1860-1930). He developed instruments that were sensitive to a plane's movements. If the plane veered off a certain flight path, the automatic pilot adjusted the controls to correct its direction.

In the 1940s, mechanical arms were used to handle dangerous chemicals behind protective screens. Today increasingly precise robots are being built. Some can be given verbal commands and respond to their surroundings.

A cutaway picture of a robotic arm used for welding

Beam

The up-and-down movement of the piston was converted into rotary (rotating) motion by a beam and a device called a sun and planet gear.

Sun and planet gear

Flywheel

This belt transferred the movement of the fly wheel to power machinery

This pump supplied cold water to the condensing system.

These hoses supply water, air and electricity to the welding gun.

The welding gun is attached to the robotic arm.

These wires supply electricity to the robot.

This joint called the "elbow" allows the arm to rotate.

This joint allows the arm to move up and down.

This is "Wabot", a Japanese-made robot with two legs. It was built to study how robots can walk and balance.

Motor cars

T he first horseless road vehicles, built at the end of the 18th century, were huge steam-powered carriages. In 1860, the invention of the internal combustion engine (see below) made smaller, fuel-driven vehicles a possibility. Since then thousands of inventions have contributed to the development of faster, cheaper, readily available motor cars. It is estimated that there are almost 500 million motor cars on the road today.

A steam-driven carriage built in 1770 by French army engineer Nicolas Cugnot

A four-stroke cycle

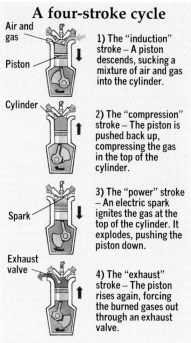

Air and gas

Piston

1) The "induction" stroke – A piston descends, sucking a mixture of air and gas into the cylinder.

Cylinder

2) The "compression" stroke – The piston is pushed back up, compressing the gas in the top of the cylinder.

Spark

3) The "power" stroke – An electric spark ignites the gas at the top of the cylinder. It explodes, pushing the piston down.

Exhaust valve

4) The "exhaust" stroke – The piston rises again, forcing the burned gases out through an exhaust valve.

Horseless carriages

The first lightweight engine was built in 1860 by Étienne Lenoir (1822-1900), a Belgian engineer. It is called an internal combustion engine because a mixture of air and coal gas was burned in a tube (called a cylinder) inside the engine. The power produced by the burning gases moved a piston which, in turn, rotated the wheels. Lenoir attached his engine to an old cart and drove down a dirt track in a wood.

In 1876, Nikolaus Otto (1832-91), a German engineer, produced a "four-stroke" engine, which takes its name from the four movements made by the piston inside the engine (see panel). Most modern motor car engines are based on Otto's design.

Lenoir's gas engine

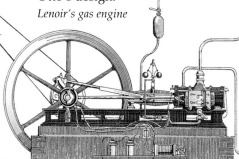

Benz

The first motor car ever sold was produced by Karl Benz (1844-1929). He developed an internal combustion engine which ran on gasoline. The vehicle he attached it to had three wheels and a horseshoe-shaped steel frame. Benz tested his vehicle in 1885, and it reached a speed of 14.5km/h (9mph).

Benz's gasoline-driven car

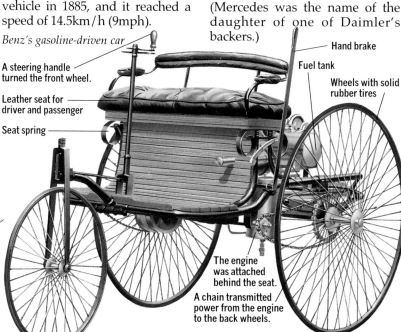

A steering handle turned the front wheel.

Leather seat for driver and passenger

Seat spring

Hand brake

Fuel tank

Wheels with solid rubber tires

The engine was attached behind the seat.

A chain transmitted power from the engine to the back wheels.

Daimler

In 1885, Gottlieb Daimler (1834-1900) and Wilhelm Maybach (1846-1929), two German engineers, developed a lightweight, high speed engine to run on gasoline. They attached it to a wooden bicycle, and created the first motorbike. By 1889, they had produced the first four-wheeled motor car. Its wheels were turned by a belt-drive mechanism.

Daimler's car

It had a steering column and a four-speed gearbox. Daimler also developed the carburetor, which mixes the air and gasoline vapor that ignites in the cylinders, making an engine run more efficiently. Daimler set up the Daimler Motor Company in 1890, which he then merged with the Benz Company in 1926 to form Mercedes–Benz. (Mercedes was the name of the daughter of one of Daimler's backers.)

Mass production

At the beginning of the 20th century, cars were still extremely expensive because they were built by hand for individual customers. Henry Ford (1863-1947), born into a farming family in Michigan, believed that reducing the price of cars would greatly increase public demand for them. In 1903, he set up his own business called the Ford Motor Company. He standardized the components from which cars were constructed and introduced the idea of a moving assembly-line to build his cars. A car was moved from one worker to the next, each of whom performed a simple task in its construction.

The first mass-produced car, the Ford Model T, rolled off the production line in 1908. By 1913, 1,000 cars were being produced each day.

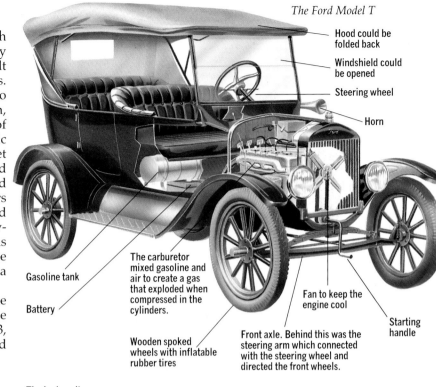

The Ford Model T

Hood could be folded back

Windshield could be opened

Steering wheel

Horn

Gasoline tank

The carburetor mixed gasoline and air to create a gas that exploded when compressed in the cylinders.

Battery

Fan to keep the engine cool

Starting handle

Wooden spoked wheels with inflatable rubber tires

Front axle. Behind this was the steering arm which connected with the steering wheel and directed the front wheels.

The assembly line of the Ford Model T

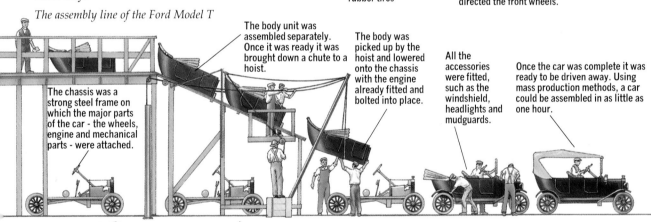

The chassis was a strong steel frame on which the major parts of the car - the wheels, engine and mechanical parts - were attached.

The body unit was assembled separately. Once it was ready it was brought down a chute to a hoist.

The body was picked up by the hoist and lowered onto the chassis with the engine already fitted and bolted into place.

All the accessories were fitted, such as the windshield, headlights and mudguards.

Once the car was complete it was ready to be driven away. Using mass production methods, a car could be assembled in as little as one hour.

Racing cars

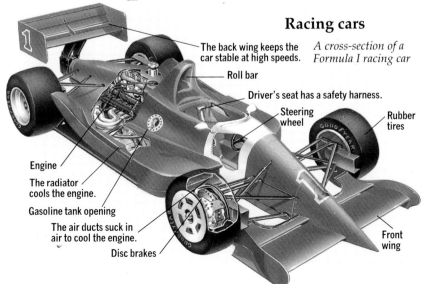

The back wing keeps the car stable at high speeds.

A cross-section of a Formula I racing car

Roll bar

Driver's seat has a safety harness.

Steering wheel

Rubber tires

Engine

The radiator cools the engine.

Gasoline tank opening

The air ducts suck in air to cool the engine.

Disc brakes

Front wing

Racing cars incorporate the latest technology in the motor industry. This technology is often later adapted and used in ordinary cars. For example, disc brakes and turbochargers were first tested on racing cars.

The bodies of racing cars are built of ultra light materials such as carbon fiber. A low, streamlined design reduces wind resistance when the car is traveling at high speed. This also means that less power and gasoline are needed to drive the car.

Trains and railways

The age of railways began at the end of the 18th century, with the invention of the steam engine and the introduction of cast iron rails. At that time, many people believed that it was dangerous to travel faster than the speed of a galloping horse, and opposed the development of locomotives.

Rail tracks were first used in mines to transport coal.

The first steam locomotive

An English mining engineer named Richard Trevithick (1771-1833) realized that steam engines could be used to propel vehicles along tracks. In 1804, he introduced the *New Castle*, the first steam locomotive ever to run on rails. It pulled wagons containing 70 passengers, and ten freight

The Catch Me Who Can, a locomotive built in 1808 by Trevithick

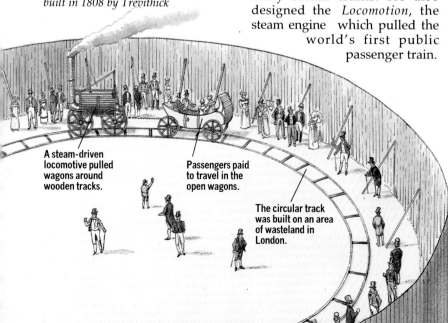

A steam-driven locomotive pulled wagons around wooden tracks.

Passengers paid to travel in the open wagons.

The circular track was built on an area of wasteland in London.

containers, along a track almost 16km (10 miles) long. It could travel at a top speed of 8km/h (5mph).

A new railway age

One of the most famous early railway engineers was George Stephenson (1781-1848), an Englishman. He was a fireman in a coal mine and a very skilled mechanic. The owner of the mine where he worked asked him to build a locomotive to carry coal.

In 1814, he produced the *Blucher*, a steam engine that could pull a weight of 30.5 tonnes (30 tons) at a speed of 6.5km/h (4mph). But it took a long time for the engine to build up enough power to move.

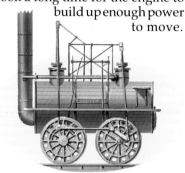

George Stephenson's Locomotion

Stephenson worked hard on improving both locomotives and the rails they ran on. In 1825, he built the first public railway to carry steam trains. He also designed the *Locomotion*, the steam engine which pulled the world's first public passenger train.

Stephenson's Rocket

Locomotives quickly became an important means of transport. In 1829, the directors of the Liverpool and Manchester Railway offered a prize for the best steam locomotive. Stephenson and his son, Robert (1803-59) won the competition with an engine called the *Rocket*, capable of speeds of up to 48km/h (30mph).

Stephenson's Rocket pulling a passenger wagon.

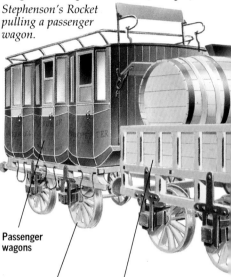

Passenger wagons

The wheels were made of wood with metal rims.

The tender carried coal for the fire and a barrel of water for making the steam.

The advantages of electricity

Some inventors investigated the possibility of building trains powered by electricity. In 1879, Ernst von Siemens (1816-92), a German electrical engineer, exhibited a train that ran on a 274m (300yd) long electrified track. Electric trains are quieter, safer and cause less pollution than steam trains.

Soon Germany and Britain had built tramways. Carriages called trams ran along tracks, powered by electricity. The use of electric railways gradually spread worldwide.

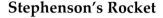

A goods train on the Liverpool and Manchester Railway

The *Rocket* pulled a 14.2 tonne (14 ton) train at nearly twice the speed of rival designs. It proved that steam power was superior to horse power and laid the foundations for the expansion of railways throughout the 19th century. Fast trains went into service on the Liverpool and Manchester Railway in September 1830, transporting passengers and heavy goods.

The boiler had 25 heating tubes leading to it from the fire box. These turned the water in the boiler into steam, which made the train powerful and fast.

Chimney

Piston driven by steam

ROCKET

An iron fire box heated metal tubes running through the water in the boiler.

Driving wheel with a connecting rod.

Underground railways

In 1863, the Metropolitan Railway was opened in London. It was the first underground railway system, using steam locomotives to pull passenger wagons.

The opening of London's Metropolitan Railway in January 1863

An early steam locomotive used on the Metropolitan Railway

The first electric underground railway was opened in London in 1890. The line ran under the River Thames joining the north and south of the city. Today many cities throughout the world have underground railways.

A cutaway picture showing the Train à Grande Vitesse (TGV) which is a high-speed, electrically powered, French passenger train.

Driver's cab

Brake gear

Collision protection

Cooling air vents

Traction motors

This frame connects the train with overhead wires

Baggage compartment

Passenger compartment

Battery compartments

Air conditioning system

Suspension

A bogie is a trolley with four wheels. It swivels to steer the train around bends. These bogies have an elaborate suspension system to provide a very smooth ride.

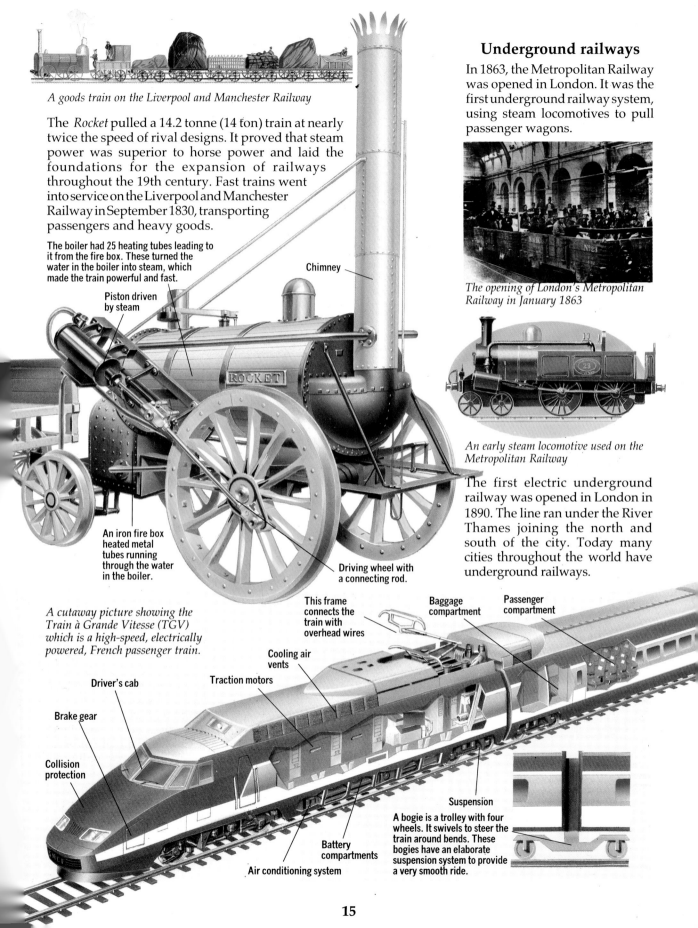

Sea transport

The first sailors used trees, grass and animal skins to build rafts and canoes. But as sea transport became essential for communication and trade, stronger and faster ships were needed. In time, wooden sailing ships were replaced by vessels made of iron and later of steel. The invention of the steam engine (see page 10) meant that ships no longer had to rely on oars, wind or tides for power.

Steam power

Frenchman Claude Marquis de Jouffroy d'Abbans (1751-1832) built the first steamboat, called the *Pyroscape*, in 1783. The boat had a steam engine which turned its paddle wheels.

In 1836, an English farmer named Francis Pettit Smith (1803-74) designed a screw propeller. It had curved blades which propelled a boat forward by pushing water backward. Unlike a paddle wheel, a propeller stayed under water and was less easily damaged.

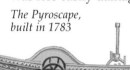

The Pyroscape, built in 1783

Revolutionary ship design

Isambard Kingdom Brunel (1806-59), an English engineer, revolutionized ship design. In 1837, he designed the *Great Western*, the largest wooden ship of its time and the first steamship to sail across the Atlantic regularly.

Brunel's next vessel, the *Great Britain*, was driven by a huge screw propeller and built of iron, making it very strong.

Brunel's largest ship was the *Great Eastern*. It was designed to transport 4,000 passengers in great luxury and carry enough coal to sail from England to Australia and back. It was launched in 1858, but there was an explosion on board, and it proved too expensive to run. Brunel died soon after the launch, overworked and financially ruined. The *Great Eastern* was sold for scrap 30 years later.

Isambard Kingdom Brunel

Submarines

In the 17th century, one of the first boats to travel under water was built for King James I of England by Cornelius Van Drebbel (c.1572-1633), a Dutchman.

The Nautilus was built in 1800. It was driven under water by a hand-cranked propeller and above water by a sail.

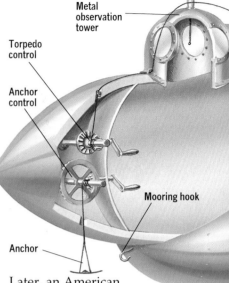

Metal observation tower

Torpedo control

Anchor control

Mooring hook

Anchor

Later, an American engineer and inventor named Robert Fulton (1765-1815) designed the *Nautilus* for Emperor Napoleon I of France. This submarine could carry four passengers and remain submersed for three hours.

The first naval submarine was designed by an Irish engineer named John Holland (1840-1914). In 1900, he made the *Holland VI*, which had an internal combustion engine for travel above water and an electric motor for moving underwater.

A cutaway diagram of the Ben Franklin, a modern research submarine

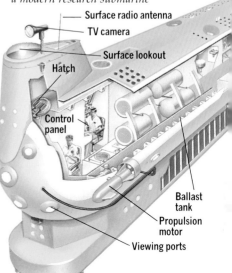

Surface radio antenna

TV camera

Surface lookout

Hatch

Control panel

Ballast tank

Propulsion motor

Viewing ports

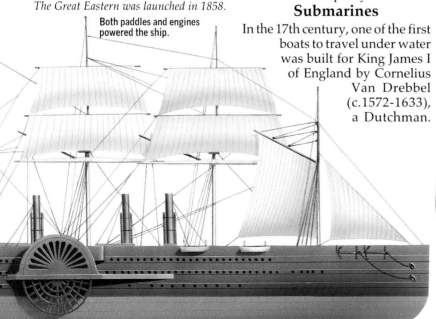

The Great Eastern was launched in 1858.

Both paddles and engines powered the ship.

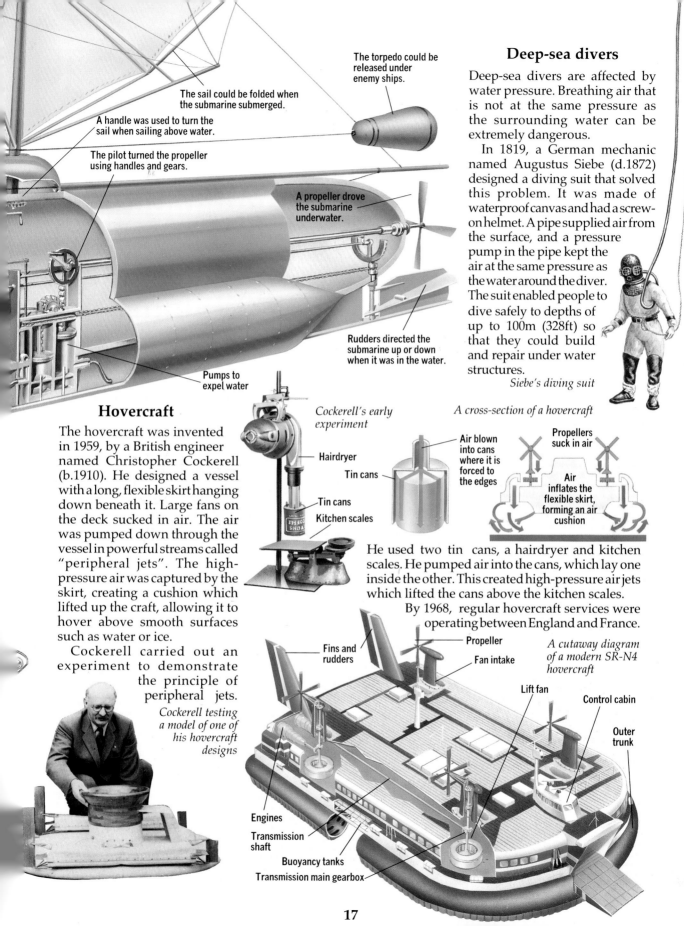

The sail could be folded when the submarine submerged.

A handle was used to turn the sail when sailing above water.

The pilot turned the propeller using handles and gears.

The torpedo could be released under enemy ships.

A propeller drove the submarine underwater.

Rudders directed the submarine up or down when it was in the water.

Pumps to expel water

Deep-sea divers

Deep-sea divers are affected by water pressure. Breathing air that is not at the same pressure as the surrounding water can be extremely dangerous.

In 1819, a German mechanic named Augustus Siebe (d.1872) designed a diving suit that solved this problem. It was made of waterproof canvas and had a screw-on helmet. A pipe supplied air from the surface, and a pressure pump in the pipe kept the air at the same pressure as the water around the diver. The suit enabled people to dive safely to depths of up to 100m (328ft) so that they could build and repair under water structures.

Siebe's diving suit

Hovercraft

The hovercraft was invented in 1959, by a British engineer named Christopher Cockerell (b.1910). He designed a vessel with a long, flexible skirt hanging down beneath it. Large fans on the deck sucked in air. The air was pumped down through the vessel in powerful streams called "peripheral jets". The high-pressure air was captured by the skirt, creating a cushion which lifted up the craft, allowing it to hover above smooth surfaces such as water or ice.

Cockerell carried out an experiment to demonstrate the principle of peripheral jets.

Cockerell's early experiment

Hairdryer

Tin cans

Tin cans

Kitchen scales

A cross-section of a hovercraft

Propellers suck in air

Air blown into cans where it is forced to the edges

Air inflates the flexible skirt, forming an air cushion

He used two tin cans, a hairdryer and kitchen scales. He pumped air into the cans, which lay one inside the other. This created high-pressure air jets which lifted the cans above the kitchen scales.

By 1968, regular hovercraft services were operating between England and France.

Cockerell testing a model of one of his hovercraft designs

Fins and rudders

Propeller

Fan intake

Lift fan

Control cabin

Outer trunk

A cutaway diagram of a modern SR-N4 hovercraft

Engines

Transmission shaft

Buoyancy tanks

Transmission main gearbox

Air transport

The idea of being able to fly has captured people's imagination from the earliest times. In Greek mythology, a man called Icarus tried to fly to the Sun with wings made of feathers and wax. But hot air balloons, the first successful way of flying, were not built until the 18th century. Aircraft were invented in the 20th century and soon revolutionized both transport and warfare.

Balloon flight

Balloons filled with hot air float because hot air is lighter than cold air. The first successful hot air balloon was built in France in 1783 by the Montgolfier brothers, Joseph (1740-1810) and Jacques (1745-99).

The balloon was made from paper pasted onto linen.

A sheep, a duck and a cockerel were among the first passengers. They flew for about eight minutes, covering only a short distance. The first balloon flight with human passengers lasted about 25 minutes and covered a distance of 8km (5 miles).

Later, instead of hot air, balloons were filled with gases that are lighter than air, such as hydrogen. Ballooning became a very popular sport. But when one of the first balloons crash landed, the people who found it thought it was a monster and tried to kill it.

Long-distance balloons

Balloons were very difficult to steer. They often blew a long way off course, or climbed so high above the Earth's surface that pilots had difficulty breathing. In 1852, Frenchman Henri Giffard (1825-82) designed an "airship", a balloon 44m (144ft) in length and pointed at each end. It was steered by a propeller, and driven by a steam engine.

In 1898, Ferdinand von Zeppelin (1838-1917) built an airship with a rigid frame inside made of a lightweight metal. After this, huge airships were built for passenger trips. One, the *Graf Zeppelin*, made 144 transatlantic flights. But in 1937, 35 people were killed when the world's largest balloon, the *Hindenburg*, caught fire. Airships were taken out of service shortly after this.

Wooden struts supported the wings.

Twin rudders at the rear gave directional control.

Gun platform

Observation and gun platform

Observation platform

Winch platform

Bow cabins

Control car

Aircraft compartment

Helium gas cell

Metal frames

An American airship. In Europe, airships were converted into bombers in World War I and carried out air-raids, dropping bombs on London.

A pioneer of flight

A flying machine which successfully imitated a bird's flight was built by a rich English landowner, Sir George Cayley (1771-1857). In 1853 he launched a glider, piloted by his coachman, from a hilltop on his estate in Yorkshire.

Otto Lilienthal (1849-96), a German engineer, made over a thousand flights in monoplane (single-wing) and biplane (double-wing) gliders that he had designed and built. But he was eventually killed when one of his gliders crashed.

The pilot hung below the glider and moved his body and legs to control the direction of flight.

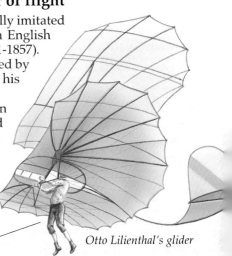

Otto Lilienthal's glider

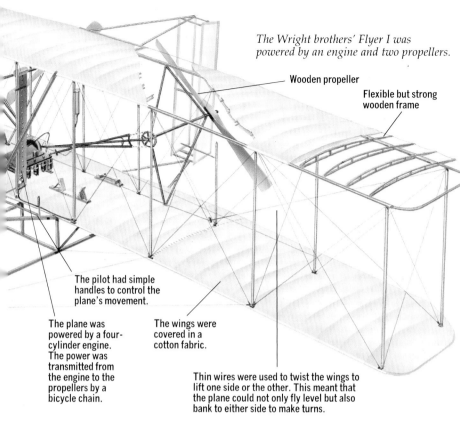

The Wright brothers' Flyer I was powered by an engine and two propellers.

Wooden propeller

Flexible but strong wooden frame

The pilot had simple handles to control the plane's movement.

The plane was powered by a four-cylinder engine. The power was transmitted from the engine to the propellers by a bicycle chain.

The wings were covered in a cotton fabric.

Thin wires were used to twist the wings to lift one side or the other. This meant that the plane could not only fly level but also bank to either side to make turns.

The first aircraft flights

Orville (1871-1948) and Wilbur (1867-1912) Wright were the sons of an American bishop. They designed an extremely lightweight engine and fitted it to their first aircraft, *Flyer I*.

On December 17, 1903, Orville Wright piloted the first powered and controlled aircraft flight. He made four flights that day. The longest lasted 59 seconds and covered a distance of 260m (852ft). *Flyer III*, built in 1905, was the first efficient plane. It could fly for over half an hour, and was easy to steer and control. In 1909, the American army recognized the importance of the Wright brothers' achievement and ordered a military version of the plane.

Wilbur Wright in Flyer III

From aircraft to helicopters

Igor Sikorsky (1889-1972) was an engineer who emigrated to America from Russia. In 1939, he built the first modern helicopter, *Sikorsky VS-300*. Like helicopters today, it had a single main propeller called a rotor and a small tail propeller. It was able to take off and land vertically, fly backwards and sideways, and hover.

The Sikorsky VS-300

Defying gravity

In the 17th century, the British scientist Isaac Newton (1642-1727) predicted that it would be possible to launch an object into space. Two hundred years later Konstantin Tsiolkovsky (1857-1933), a Russian school teacher, calculated that a rocket would have to travel at about 40,250km/h (25,000mph) to leave the Earth's atmosphere. He realized that if certain liquid fuels were mixed and ignited, the explosion could propel a rocket into space at such a speed. In 1926, the first liquid fuel rocket was launched by an American named Robert Goddard (1882-1945).

Space travel was made possible by the work of a German engineer, Baron Wernher von Braun (1912-77). During World War II, he designed a number of rockets, including the V-2 missile. It could travel at a speed of 1.6km (1 mile) per second, to a target over 322km (200 miles) away (see page 41).

After the war, von Braun worked on the American space project. In 1958, he built a system called *Jupiter* which launched the USA's first satellite (see page 29).

The Space Shuttle, launched in 1977, was the first reusable spacecraft.

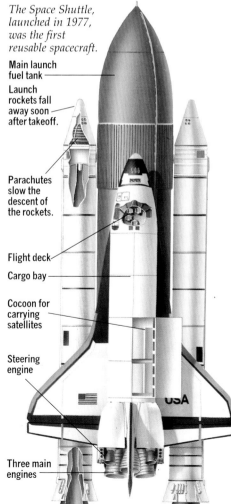

Main launch fuel tank

Launch rockets fall away soon after takeoff.

Parachutes slow the descent of the rockets.

Flight deck

Cargo bay

Cocoon for carrying satellites

Steering engine

Three main engines

Inventions in the home

In the 20th century, many inventions have transformed life in the home. Standards of hygiene have risen with the introduction of new ways of storing and preserving food. Exhausting tasks which had previously been performed by hand are now quickly completed using a variety of electrical devices.

Electric irons

The first irons were metal pans, filled with hot charcoal. They were used in the 8th century by the Chinese to smooth silk. In the 17th century, pieces of cast iron fitted with handles were heated on a fire or stove. In 1882, Henry Seely, an American, made an iron that had an electric element.

An early electric iron

Electric element

High-powered cleaning

Up until the 19th century, people had to clean their carpets by beating or washing them. The first mechanical carpet cleaners were sweepers with rotating brushes, or devices fitted with bellows to suck up dust.

The first successful vacuum cleaner was invented by Hubert Booth (1871-1955), a British engineer, who set up the British Vacuum Company in 1901. His fuel-driven machine, known as the "Puffing Billy", was taken from house to house by a horse-drawn van. Uniformed employees put hoses through windows to clean people's carpets. Booth's machine was such a success that he was asked to clean the ceremonial carpet at Westminster Abbey, London, before the coronation of King Edward VII of England.

In 1908, an American named Murray Spangler patented a new lightweight vacuum cleaner. His design was eventually made and marketed by a firm owned by William Hoover.

An early Hoover "bag and stick" vacuum cleaner

An electric motor turned a large fan, creating a vacuum inside the Hoover. The vacuum sucked in dirt and dust off the carpet, which was collected in a large bag at the back.

A brush at the front picked up and pushed back dirt.

On/off switch

Keeping cool

Food which is kept cool lasts longer than food left at room temperature. People often used ice to preserve things until Karl von Linde (1842-1934), a German inventor, made the first domestic refrigerator. It was powered by a steam motor which pumped a gas called freon into pipes behind a food cabinet. Inside the pipes the gas condensed into a liquid. As this happened, the temperature of the freon dropped, cooling down the food cabinet.

The first electric refrigerator was designed in 1923 by two Swedish inventors, Balzer von Platen and Carl Munters.

A cutaway of a modern refrigerator

Evaporator absorbs heat from the air

Freezer compartment

Cooled air at the top sinks to the bottom; warmer air rises to be cooled.

Compressor

Condenser

A compressor pumps freon gas around the refrigerator inside pipes. When it reaches the condenser it is condensed into a liquid. Its temperature drops, cooling the refrigerator.

A close shave

The first safety razor, in which only the edge of the blade touched the skin, was made in 1771, by Jean-Jacques Perret, a Frenchman. Before this, blades were unshielded, making shaving dangerous. King Camp Gillette (1855-1932), an American salesman, had the idea of a razor blade which was thrown away when blunt. With an inventor, William Nickerson, he patented the disposable safety razor in 1901. In 1908, 300,000 razors and 13 million blades were sold.

An early disposable razor

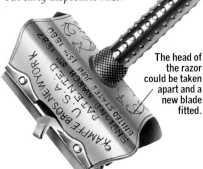

The head of the razor could be taken apart and a new blade fitted.

Electric toaster

In 1909, the General Electric Company of the USA produced the first electric toaster. A slice of bread was placed on a mesh of wires heated by an electric current. The bread had to be turned over when one side was done, to toast the other side.

An American named Charles Strite designed the first pop-up toaster in 1927. It had heating elements to toast both sides of the bread at once. A clockwork timer turned off the electricity and, at the same time, released a spring which ejected the toast.

An electric toaster, dating from 1938

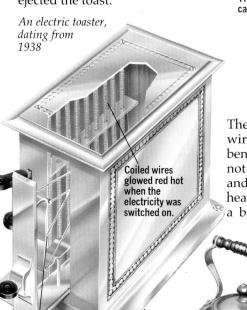

Coiled wires glowed red hot when the electricity was switched on.

The bread was placed here and pushed into the toaster.

Washing machines

The world's first electric washing machine was built in 1906 by an American, named Alva Fisher. Dirty clothes were placed in a horizontally-mounted metal drum, which was rotated by an electric motor. As the clothes tumbled they gradually became clean. The first combined electric washer and tumble dryer was introduced in 1924 by the Savage Arms Co. of the USA.

A modern tumble dryer

Heating element

Drum

Hot air is pumped into the rotating drum. This heats the water held in the clothes causing it to evaporate.

An electric motor turns the drum

A condenser unit dries the moisture in the air inside the drum.

Pump

Electric kettles

The first electric kettles contained wires in separate compartments beneath their bases. The water did not come into contact with the wire and therefore took a long time to heat up. In 1923, Arthur Large made a breakthrough. He developed a copper tube containing a wire that could safely be covered by water in a kettle. It heated water quickly.

An electric kettle made in about 1920

Electric element

Canned food

Food preserved in tin canisters was introduced by an Englishman named Peter Durand. His idea was bought by a company called Donkin, Hall and Gamble. They set up a canning factory in 1811 and canned foods were sold in London shops by 1830.

This can of roast veal was taken on an expedition to the Arctic in 1824. When scientists opened it 114 years later, the meat was in perfect condition.

Microwave ovens

In 1945, the idea of making an oven which used radio waves to heat up food was patented by an American inventor named Percy Spencer. In a microwave oven, food is bombarded with radio waves, called microwaves. These make the molecules inside the food vibrate, producing heat which cooks the food quickly.

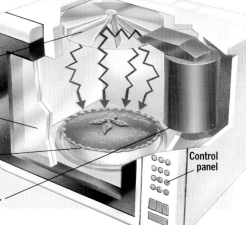

A modern microwave oven

The microwaves are directed onto a fan. This spins around and spreads the waves throughout the oven.

A special metal mesh across the oven door prevents the microwaves from escaping, but allows the food to be viewed safely.

A turntable rotates so that the food will be cooked evenly.

The microwaves are generated in a vacuum tube called a magnetron.

Control panel

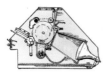

A revolution in the office

W ith the mass-production of a selection of tiny electronic components, many sophisticated devices have become commonplace in offices. Word processors, photocopiers and facsimile machines have simplified business transactions all over the world. This new equipment also enables more and more people to work from home.

Mechanical writing

The first practical typewriter was designed in 1867, by Christopher Sholes (1819-90 an American newspaper editor and politician. He spent much of his spare time inventing. With his friend Carlos Glidden, he invented a numbering machine, which they later decided to convert into a lettering machine.

Sholes built about 30 different machines and designed a keyboard layout similar to that used today. But he did not make money out of his invention. He sold it to a company named Remington and Sons, who sold their first type-writer in 1874. Typewriters soon became very popular. The author Mark Twain, an early enthusiast, typed his own manuscripts.

An early Sholes typewriter

Personal computers

In 1964, a US company called IBM produced the first word processor. It was a typewriter with a computer memory that could store text on magnetic tapes. When a tape was played back, the typewriter printed out the text. In 1978, another US company, called Qyx, introduced a machine which used magnetic disks to store text. These disks could store more information than the tapes, and allowed the user to retrieve stored information quickly.

In the 1980s, personal computers running special word processing programs began to replace typewriters. Today computers can be used to produce many types of publications, such as this book, to keep accounts and to store and organize huge amounts of office information of all kinds.

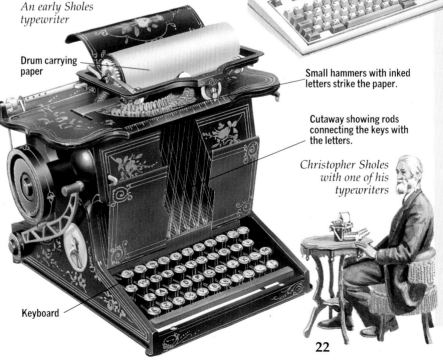

A modern personal computer

Monitor

System unit, inside which are the workings of the computer

Floppy disk drive into which floppy disks can be inserted.

Hard disk drive

Graphics card

Keyboard

Mouse

Drum carrying paper

Small hammers with inked letters strike the paper.

Cutaway showing rods connecting the keys with the letters.

Christopher Sholes with one of his typewriters

Keyboard

Paper clips

The paper clip was invented in 1900 by Johann Vaaler of Norway. The design, which has remained almost the same ever since, consisted of a simple double loop of wire which could hold sheets of paper tightly together. Before, loose pieces of paper had to be pinned together.

Sticky tape

In 1928, Richard Drew an American, produced a general-purpose sticky tape. It was known as "Scotch tape", but in Europe it was sold under the name "Sellotape". It consisted of a strip of clear plastic called cellulose, with glue on one side.

Photocopying

In 1938, an American inventor named Chester Carlson (1906-68) invented the xerographic copier, now known as the photocopier. Modern photocopiers work in the following way:

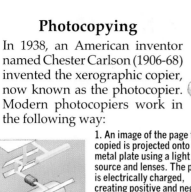

1. An image of the page to be copied is projected onto a metal plate using a light source and lenses. The plate is electrically charged, creating positive and negative charges on its surface.

2. Light areas of the image destroy the positive charges on the plate. Where the image is dark, the positive charges remain. The plate is then coated with toner powder.

3. The toner powder sticks to the positively charged areas of the metal plate. It is then transferred onto a sheet of paper which comes from the feed tray.

4. The toner powder is then sealed onto the sheet of paper as it passes between two heated fusing rollers.

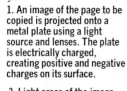

Chester Carlson with his invention

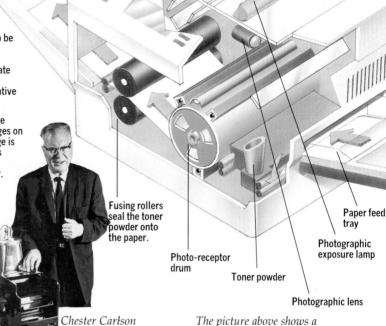

Mirrors

Fusing rollers seal the toner powder onto the paper.

Photo-receptor drum

Toner powder

Paper feed tray

Photographic exposure lamp

Photographic lens

The picture above shows a cutaway of a modern photocopier

Facsimile transmission

A facsimile (fax) machine can transmit text and photographs by telephone to a receiving machine a few seconds later. The first fax machine appeared in 1843. It consisted of a pendulum which scanned raised lettering and sent out electrical pulses. Modern machines use diodes (see page 32) which detect light reflected from the document being sent.

In 1922, Arthur Korn, a German physicist, sent photographs by radio transmission across the Atlantic. The first fax service was set up in 1926.

How a modern fax machine works

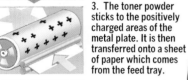

1. The document to be faxed is fed in here.

2. A fluorescent tube bounces light off the document, reflecting its image onto a lens.

3. The lens passes the light to a microprocessor. This breaks the image down into a series of lines.

4. The lines are then changed by another microprocessor into white and black dots. These are converted into a number code - "1" for white and "0" for black.

5. Another microprocessor converts this information into signals which are sent down a telephone line.

6. At the receiving fax machine, the telephone message is converted back to a number code.

7. The code is sent to a printer, which contains a line of dots which heat up or cool down according to the electrical current supplied by the number code.

8. An image of black dots is formed on a piece of paper, matching the information given by the code.

The ballpoint pen

In 1938, a design for the first ballpoint pen was patented by Lazlo Biro (1900-85) a Hungarian artist and journalist, and his brother Georg, a chemist. They called their pen the biro. Ink from a reservoir inside the pen flowed onto a free-moving steel ball.

A special ink was invented for use in ballpoint pens. It dried instantly when it was exposed to air. The pen was first used by the British Royal Air Force, because it did not leak at high altitudes.

A ballpoint pen, 1940s

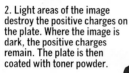

Ink in a plastic tube

Ink flows onto a small metal ball.

Construction and buildings

In the 18th and 19th centuries, millions of people left rural areas to work in the world's growing industrial cities. Many traditional building methods had to change in order to provide accommodation for the new urban population. The work of many inventors enabled architects to design and construct much bigger, brighter and safer buildings.

Cranes

The earliest description of a crane appears in a handbook written in about 10BC by the Roman architect Vitruvius. It consisted of a pole held in position by ropes, with a pulley at the top. A rope running through the pulley was attached to heavy loads such as building materials or ships' cargoes. The loads were then lifted by slaves in a treadmill.

The crane described by Vitruvius

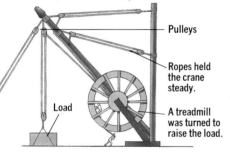

- Pulleys
- Ropes held the crane steady.
- Load
- A treadmill was turned to raise the load.

A more efficient crane, known as the derrick crane, was designed in Italy during the 15th century. Steam-powered cranes were built in the 19th century by a Scots engineer named John Rennie (1761-1821).

Building the Tower of Babel – an illustration of the mythical tower, from an English book published in 1425

A bucket being raised with ropes and pulleys

Elevators for high-rise buildings

During the 19th century, architects designed such tall buildings that machinery was needed to transport people and goods up and down them. Elisha Otis (1811-61) was an engineer from Vermont. In 1852 he took a job in a factory in New York, where he designed a steam-powered safety elevator. It included a spring operated safety mechanism to hold the passenger platform securely if the elevator cables broke. Otis demonstrated his new invention to the public. He was lifted high up in the air in an elevator and then its cables were cut. In 1857, the first safety elevator was installed in a New York department store.

Elevators were installed at the Eiffel Tower in Paris in 1889.

- Ticket collector
- Passengers going up a leg of the Eiffel Tower.
- A driver controlled the speed.
- Elevator controls
- One of the elevators carried sightseers up 160m (146ft) to a viewing platform.
- The elevator was hydraulically powered, which means the car was pushed up rails using a liquid under pressure.

Moving staircases

In 1894, the world's first escalator was installed as a tourist attraction on a pier at Coney Island, New York. It was named the "inclined elevator" and was designed by Jesse Reno, a businessman from New York. A conveyor belt pulled around a sloping ramp. But the ramp sloped at an angle of about 30 degrees to the ground, which made it dangerous for passengers. So Reno replaced the ramp with a set of rotating steps.

In the early 1980s, a Japanese company named Mitsubishi built the first spiral escalator. It was installed in a department store.

Toilets

As the population in cities increased, a hygienic way of disposing of sewage was urgently needed. In 1778, Joseph Bramah (1748-1814), an English cabinet maker whose job was fitting water closets (an early kind of toilet), designed and patented a new toilet. A valve shut the toilet off from the main sewer pipes when it was not in use. This stopped poisonous gases from seeping into houses.

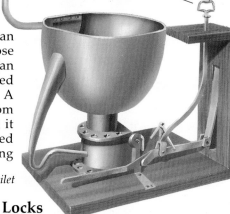

Lifting this handle opened two flaps. One flushed water into the bowl, and the other let it drain away.

Bramah's toilet

Locks

Bramah also invented a complex lock. He offered a reward to anyone who could open it. 75 years later, at London's Great Exhibition of 1851 (a fair at which the world's newest technology was shown), a visitor finally picked it open; even then it took 51 hours.

Locks were first used in Ancient Egypt. They were made of wood and were opened using a key. The key had cylindrical pins of different lengths which fitted into grooves in the lock. Inspired by the Egyptian ideas, Linus Yale (1821-68) produced a modern pin lock, known as a Yale lock.

Bramah's original lock of 1787

How a Yale lock works

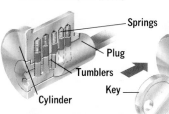

Springs

Plug

Tumblers

Key

Cylinder

The lock consists of a brass cylinder with a central plug, both with a row of holes. In each hole is a moveable pin made in two pieces called a tumbler. Springs hold down the tumblers.

The key has a serrated top edge. When it is inserted, it pushes up each tumbler against its spring so the holes in the tumbler align with the edge of the central plug.

When the key is turned, the central plug also turns. A lever attached to the central plug draws in a bolt and the lock opens.

Gas lamps

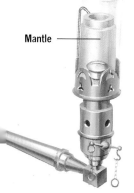

Mantle

Most early gas lamps were simply holes in gas pipes. When lit, the escaping gas gave off a very weak light. In 1885, an Austrian chemist, Carl Auer (1858-1929), designed a new kind of gas lamp. It contained a device known as a mantle, which consisted of a mesh of carbonized cotton that glowed brightly when heated in a gas flame.

Auer's gas mantle of 1885

Electric lighting

In 1878, an English scientist named Joseph Swan (1828-1914) invented an electric light bulb. It consisted of a glass bulb containing a filament made of carbonized cotton. He removed air from the bulb, because without air the filament would never burn away.

The following year, Thomas Edison (1847-1931), a prolific inventor from the USA, also produced a light bulb. After experimenting with filaments of carbonized thread, he used carbonized paper filaments. In 1880, he began manufacturing light bulbs that were safe to use in houses, and sold them for $2.50 each. Eventually Thomas Edison combined forces with Swan to form the Edison and Swan United Electric Light Company.

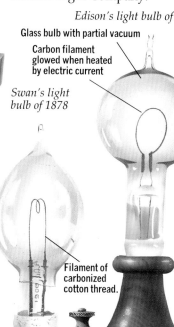

Edison's light bulb of 1879

Glass bulb with partial vacuum

Carbon filament glowed when heated by electric current

Swan's light bulb of 1878

Filament of carbonized cotton thread.

Edison with his light bulb

Printing

Before printing was invented, texts had to be copied out by people called scribes. Only a small number of books could be produced, which made them very expensive. In one day, a printer could produce the amount of material that a scribe took a whole year to complete. Books and pamphlets became widely available, and knowledge and new ideas spread more quickly.

Blocks and types

The first printed pages were prayer sheets, produced in Japan in the 8th century. They were made from blocks of wood, carved with raised characters or pictures. But each block took a long time to make, and could only be used for one page.

The Diamond Sutra, the oldest known printed book, AD868

In about 1045, Pi Cheng, a member of the royal court of China, invented movable type. He used baked clay to make single Chinese characters, which were then fitted into an iron frame ready for printing. The characters could be used again to make up new pages.

Early blocks of reusable Turkish type

Printing in Europe

In the 15th century, Johannes Gutenberg (c.1400-68), a German printer, who was unaware of the techniques used in China, developed his own version of movable type. He made individual letter blocks from metal. The letters required for each page of text were arranged in a wooden frame and fitted into a press. They were then inked and paper was pressed onto them. Thousands of copies could be printed and the type could then be rearranged for a new page.

A reconstruction of Gutenberg's press

An engraving of Johannes Gutenberg, and a page from his Bible

Conflict and loss

Gutenberg's work won him the support of Johannes Fust, a businessman. Fust was impatient for financial success. In 1455, he successfully sued Gutenberg and seized all the printing equipment.

He set up a printing business with his son-in-law, who had trained as one of Gutenberg's apprentices.

Before his death in 1468, Gutenberg saw his invention used throughout Europe and watched other people making rich profits. By 1500 there were 100 German presses in Italy, and 30 in Spain.

A wooden screw enabled the press to be raised and lowered.

Metal letters were arranged into pages in a metal frame called a forme. They were then covered in ink by a hand roller.

Padded wooden hammers were used to make all the letters level.

Paper was placed in a frame called a tympan.

The tympan hinged over the forme and both were slid under the press.

The press was screwed down so that the inked letters printed clearly onto the paper.

The steam press

By the end of the 18th century, newspapers and books had become so popular that hand-worked presses could not keep up with demand. Friedrich König (1774-1833), a printer and engineer from Saxony (now part of Germany), and his partner Andreas Bauer designed a steam-driven press. It printed 1,000 sheets an hour, four times the speed of a hand-worked press.

König's machine, produced in 1814, contained two large cylinders on which paper was placed. After one sheet had been printed on each, the cylinders rotated, bringing new blank sheets into position. The plate holding the type was automatically re-inked when necessary.

König's printing press of 1814

The press had two cylinders, so that two copies of each sheet could be printed with every backward-and-forward motion.

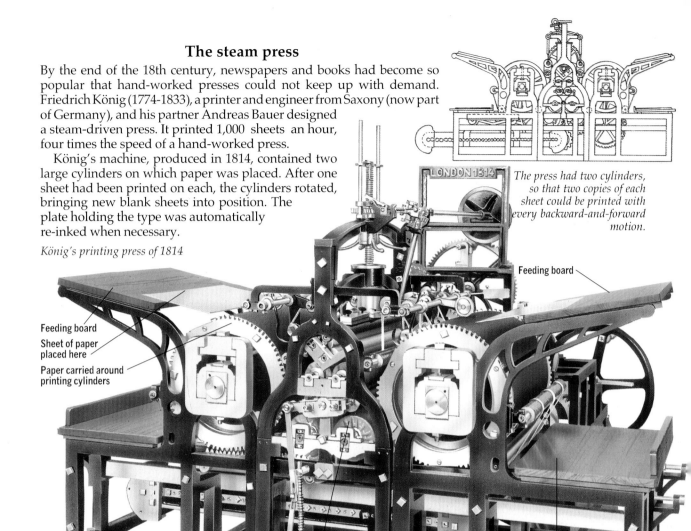

LONDON 1814

Feeding board

Feeding board

Sheet of paper placed here

Paper carried around printing cylinders

Inking rollers

Delivery table receives printed sheets

The invention of Linotype

In 1886, Ottmar Mergenthaler (1854-99), a German watchmaker, invented a way of setting type mechanically, called the Linotype system. Text was typed on a keyboard like a typewriter. The machine produced complete lines of type, with each letter and word correctly spaced, at four times the speed that was previously possible.

Mergenthaler using a Linotype machine

Computer typesetting

In 1965, a computer-controlled method of setting type, called Digiset, was developed in Germany. Text was typed on a keyboard and stored in a computer's memory. The text was then scanned by a laser and an image of the letters projected onto photographic paper, which was developed. The Digitek system of computer typesetting shown below was developed in the 1980s. Text stored in a computer's memory is scanned and converted into a code of pulses of light. An image of the text is projected onto photographic paper by the exposure head.

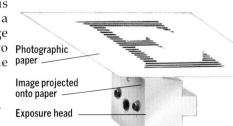

Photographic paper

Image projected onto paper

Exposure head

The Digitek system of typesetting

Communication machines

Before message-sending machines were invented in the 19th century, communication was a very slow and difficult process. People could only send letters by messengers, or signals using drums, smoke, fires, church bells and flashing mirrors. Most of these methods were only effective over a short distance, and correspondence over long distances was a very time-consuming operation. Even with the invention of steamships, it took months for a letter sent from Europe to arrive in Australia.

Communication towers

Claude Chappe (1763-1805), a Frenchman, introduced a system called the telegraph, which means "writing at a distance". A network of towers was built on hilltops. Each tower housed a machine with two long pointers that could be set in 49 different positions. Each of the positions corresponded to a letter or number. Operators could send messages from one tower to the next. The system was very successful. By the mid-19th century, the network of towers stretched at least 4,828km (3,000 miles) throughout France.

One of Chappe's towers

An alphabet called semaphore, invented in 1812

Messages along wires

The first electric telegraph machine was produced in 1837 by the British inventors William Cooke (1806-79) and Charles Wheatstone (1802-75). Electrical currents were sent along a wire to a receiving device. The currents then moved several needles that were mounted on a dial on the receiver. The needles pointed to letters, spelling out the message.

A later version of Cooke and Wheatstone's telegraph machine

Morse code

In 1843, an American artist by the name of Samuel Morse (1791-1872) designed a new telegraph code which replaced the one used by Cooke and Wheatstone. He gave every letter of the alphabet a coded equivalent of dots and dashes. When messages were transmitted, long electrical pulses stood for dashes and short pulses for dots. Morse code, as it is known, is still used today.

Morse publicized his code by erecting a telegraph wire 6km (37 miles) long, which stretched from Baltimore to Washington. He used this to transmit news of the presidential election.

In 1858, Charles Wheatstone devised a system in which an operator punched messages in Morse code onto long paper tapes which were fed through a telegraph transmitter. At the other end of the wire, a pen drew the code on to another tape, which was read and translated.

Eventually, the pen was replaced with a "sounder", which converted the dots and dashes into long and short sounds. Operators could listen to the coded message and write down the translation.

A	·—
B	—···
C	—·—·
D	—··
E	·
F	··—·
G	——·
H	····
I	··
J	·———
K	—·—
L	·—··
M	——
N	—·
O	———
P	·——·
Q	——·—
R	·—·
S	···
T	—
U	··—
V	···—
W	·——
X	—··—
Y	—·——
Z	——··

The alphabet and its equivalent in Morse code

Roller pulled tape along

Clockwork motor

Clockwork key to wind up receiver

Paper tape fed out from a reel in the drawer

Electromagnet

A message was tapped out with this key.

Morse's telegraph machine printed the dots and dashes of Morse code.

A B C D E F G   H I J   K L M   N   O P Q   R   S T U   V W X   Y Z

Spoken messages

Some inventors concentrated on producing a device that would enable people to talk over very long distances. A breakthrough was made by Alexander Graham Bell (1847-1922), a Scotsman who lived in Boston, Massachusetts. He ran a school for the deaf, and later went on to work at the city's university.

He and Thomas Watson (1854-1934), an electrical engineer, made an instrument consisting of a transmitter (or mouthpiece) and a receiver (or earpiece). The transmitter turned voice sounds into a varying electric current. This was sent along a wire to the earpiece, where it was changed back into voice sounds.

Bell's telephone - the mouthpiece and earpiece were identical devices.

Used as a mouthpiece – the speaker's voice vibrated a diaphragm, causing an electric current passing through it to vary in strength.

Diaphragm

Used as an earpiece – the varying current passed along the wire to the earpiece, which also contained a diaphragm. The electric current made the diaphragm vibrate, reproducing the voice sounds.

Bell made the first telephone call ever on March 10, 1876. He had spilled acid on his trousers and spoke to his colleague, "Mr Watson, can you come at once, I want you." The world's first telephone exchange opened in Connecticut in 1877. Operators had to connect the lines between one caller and another by hand. New York and Boston were linked by telephone in 1883.

The mouthpiece and earpiece of a Bell telephone in use

Telephones through the ages

Over the last century, the design of the telephone has undergone many changes.

A selection of different styles of telephones

An Edison receiver, 1879 – the user turned the handle while listening.

A Crossley telephone, 1880 – the user spoke into the top of the box and listened through the receiver.

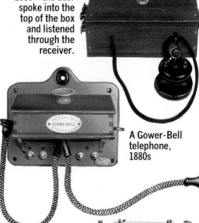

A Gower-Bell telephone, 1880s

A design introduced in the 1890s – the speaker turned the handle to call the operator.

A 'Candlestick' telephone, 1905 – the operator was called by lifting the receiver.

A 'cradle' telephone, 1930

A portable phone – these can be used without a cable.

Satellite communications

Satellites are unmanned spacecraft that orbit the Earth. They can transmit telephone calls and television pictures across the world. They can also send information about weather and navigation conditions. In 1957, the USSR launched *Sputnik I*, the first man-made object to orbit the Earth.

Sputnik I

In 1960, the USA launched the *Courier* and *Echo* satellites. They relayed the first satellite telephone calls between the USA and Europe. In 1962, the USA launched *Telstar*, the first satellite to relay live television shows as well as telephone calls. It could transmit 60 calls or a single television channel at any one time.

The Telstar satellite

Today, an elaborate network of satellites links areas all over the globe. Companies can now buy private satellites for their own communication needs.

A modern communications satellite

Solar panels power the communications system.

Communications antennae send out and receive messages.

Units for telephone and television transmissions

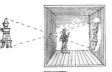

Photography and film

People have been drawing and painting the world around them since the first cave paintings. During the 10th century, Arab astronomers used an early camera obscura (see box below) to look at images of the Sun without damaging their eyes. From the 15th century, this idea was used by artists to project images onto canvases to help them draw accurately. But only the invention of the camera in the 19th century has enabled people to produce exact replicas of the things we see.

The camera obscura

The camera obscura is a box or darkened room into which light passes through a tiny pinhole, forming an image on the opposite inside wall. You can make your own camera obscura.

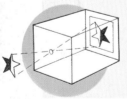

How to make a camera obscura

Make a box out of black cardboard which does not let in any light. Cut a square window into one side.

Cover the window with paper to make a screen. Make a tiny hole in the side of the box opposite the screen.

Light rays from a bright object will pass through the pinhole and form an image on the paper screen.

The first photographs

By the 18th century, people began to realize that certain chemicals are affected and changed by light. They discovered that materials coated with these substances would record patterns of light which fell across them. The world's first photograph was taken in 1826, by a French physicist named Joseph Niepce (1765-1833). He used a camera obscura to project an image onto special sheets of pewter, called plates. These had been coated with a light-sensitive substance called bitumen. It took eight hours for a blurred image to form. The length of time that light is allowed to fall on photographic plates or film is called the exposure time.

A conical camera of 1841

- Focusing dial
- Two lenses to focus the image
- The image is focused onto a screen. The camera is then dismantled and the screen replaced with a light-sensitive plate.
- A magnifying lens to help focus the image.

An early camera c.1850

Lens

Light-sensitive copper plate

Niepce's photographic techniques were improved by his partner Louis Daguerre (1789-1851). By 1839, Daguerre was obtaining clear photographs after an exposure time of only 20 minutes. His pictures were known as daguerreotypes and were very popular, particularly for portraits. But people sitting for a portrait had to have clamps around their heads to stop them from moving. The metal plates were very expensive and the pictures could not be copied.

Photography comes of age

William Fox Talbot (1800-77), an English scientist, invented a new method of developing pictures. He soaked paper in light-sensitive chemicals. When an image was projected onto the paper, the brightest areas turned it black, and the darkest parts left it white. This version of the image is called a negative. Fox Talbot then shone light through the negative onto another sheet of light-sensitive paper. This produced positive prints which he called calotypes, from the Ancient Greek words meaning "beautiful pictures".

William Fox Talbot

Photography for all

George Eastman (1854-1932), an American inventor, realized the commercial potential of making photography available to ordinary people. He produced a simple, hand-held camera called the Kodak no. 1, which was sold already fitted with a roll of film.

George Eastman's Kodak camera of 1888

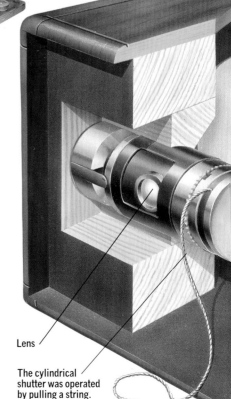

Lens

The cylindrical shutter was operated by pulling a string.

After taking one picture, the user wound the film on, ready for the next shot. When the film was finished, the camera was returned to the Eastman factory where the pictures were developed. Eastman's company motto was "You press the button, we do the rest".

Arrangement of film roll holders seen from above

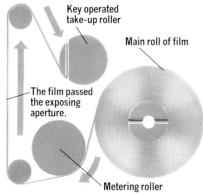

Key operated take-up roller

Main roll of film

The film passed the exposing aperture.

Metering roller

The Polaroid camera

The Polaroid camera was invented in 1947, by an American, Edwin Land (1909-91). It contained a tiny processing laboratory which produced positive black and white prints in less than one minute. The first Polaroid cameras that could take color photographs became available in 1963. Today, Polaroid cameras can develop prints in a few seconds.

Edwin Land's Polaroid camera of 1948

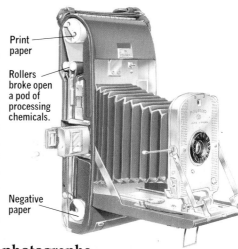

Print paper

Rollers broke open a pod of processing chemicals.

Negative paper

Sequential photographs

In 1872, Eadweard Muybridge (1830-1904), a British photographer, was hired by a Californian horse owner. To settle a bet, Muybridge was asked to discover whether a trotting horse lifts all its hooves off the ground at once. He set up 48 cameras on a racing track and rigged them to be triggered by clockwork or by threads which were broken as the horse passed. He produced the sequence of photographs shown here, which settled the bet.

Photographs from Muybridge's famous experiment

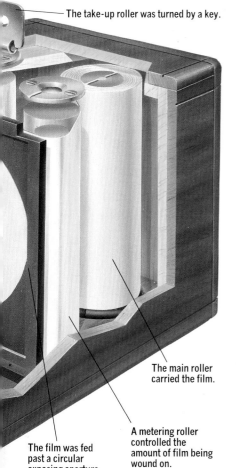

The take-up roller was turned by a key.

The main roller carried the film.

A metering roller controlled the amount of film being wound on.

The film was fed past a circular exposing aperture.

The birth of moving pictures

Any image produced in our eyes takes a moment to fade. So if many pictures of an object which is changing position are viewed in rapid succession, the brain perceives the object to be in motion. This phenomenon is called "persistent vision". It is the principle on which motion pictures work.

In 1894, two French brothers, Auguste (1862-1954) and Louis (1864-1948) Lumière, heard about the Kinetoscope, a machine invented by Thomas Edison (see page 34). It was a box containing a strip of moving photographs. When the viewer looked into the box, the objects in the pictures appeared to be moving. The brothers built a similar machine called a *Cinématographe* which projected images onto a screen. In 1895, they showed 10 films.

The first Cinématographe used in Britain

Far right: Stills from an early film of a man sneezing

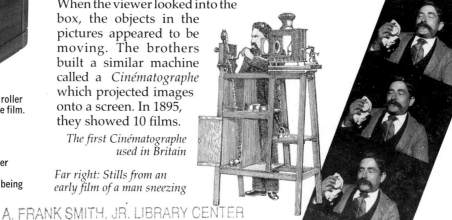

Radio and television

Unlike the telephone or telegraph, radio and television do not need cables or wires for signals to be transmitted. Today sounds and images can be sent rapidly via satellites from one side of the world to the other. This has dramatically affected communications as events can be reported around the world as soon as they happen.

Making waves

In the 19th century, scientists began to suspect that electrical and magnetic effects were transmitted in waves, like light. Heinrich Hertz (1857-94) a German scientist, proved this in 1885. He showed that the waves emitted by an electric spark on one side of his laboratory could be detected by a loop of wire on the other.

Messages without wires

Guglielmo Marconi (1874-1937), an Italian inventor, discovered a way in which waves could be used to send messages from one place to another without wires or cables. At the age of 20, having read about Hertz's work with electromagnetic waves, he began to carry out his own experiments. In 1894, he successfully sounded a buzzer 9m (30ft) away from where he stood.

Guglielmo Marconi with his wireless telegraph.

He pressed a key which was not connected by wire to the bell. The electromagnetic waves that made this happen are called radio waves.

Marconi moved to London, where he patented his ideas and demonstrated his equipment to the British Post Office, who decided to

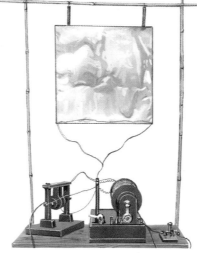
A "Marconiphone" patented in 1896

finance his work. After improving his equipment, Marconi was able to send a message in Morse code (see page 28) from England to a radio receiver 50km (31 miles) away in France.

In 1902, Marconi sent a radio signal across the Atlantic – the letter 's' in Morse code. Five years later, a Canadian scientist, Reginald Fessenden, transmitted a human voice by radio for the first time.

The Marconiphone broadcaster-receiver wireless sets (1922)

Diodes

An important contribution to the development of radio and television was made in 1904 by a British engineer named John Fleming (1849-1945), who designed the diode. Diodes are used to convert radio waves into electrical signals which can be transmitted over long distances.

Spinning discs

In 1884, Paul Nipkow (1860-1940), a German engineer, developed a disc with a spiral pattern of square holes. When the disc was rotated in front of an object, each hole captured the light from a small area of the object. These fragments could be transmitted through another disc which reformed them as a whole image on a screen. The Nipkow disc was an important step in the invention of television.

A diagram demonstrating the principle of the Nipkow disc

Light from the object passes through a spinning Nipkow disc to a photoelectric cell.

Object

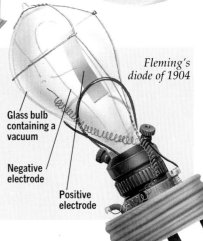
Fleming's diode of 1904

Glass bulb containing a vacuum

Negative electrode

Positive electrode

The photoelectric cell turns the energy in the light into electrical signals. These signals vary according to the amount of light falling on the cell - strong light produces a strong electrical signal and weak light produces a weak one.

The cell is linked to a lamp, which varies in brightness according to the strength of the electrical signal. This information about the light and dark areas of the object is then flashed to a second Nipkow disc.

Photoelectric cell

Lamp

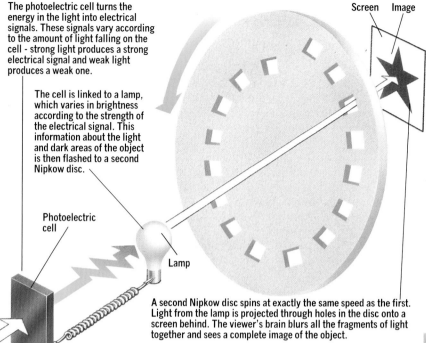

Screen   Image

A second Nipkow disc spins at exactly the same speed as the first. Light from the lamp is projected through holes in the disc onto a screen behind. The viewer's brain blurs all the fragments of light together and sees a complete image of the object.

Live television

In 1926, John Logie Baird (1888-1946), a Scottish inventor, made the first television transmission of a human face. His apparatus included an old box, a cake tin, knitting needles, a bicycle lamp and a cardboard Nipkow disc. In his laboratory, he transmitted a blurred image of the face of a boy named William Taynton. As Baird improved his equipment, the pictures he produced became less distorted. Later that year he gave the first public demonstration of television.

After this breakthrough, many television systems were developed. The British Broadcasting Corporation (BBC) began operating a black and white television service from London in 1936, and by 1939 there were television receivers in 20,000 homes. In the USA in 1953, the first successful transmission of color television was made.

A television picture of a face was achieved in 1926

Baird's transmitting equipment of 1926

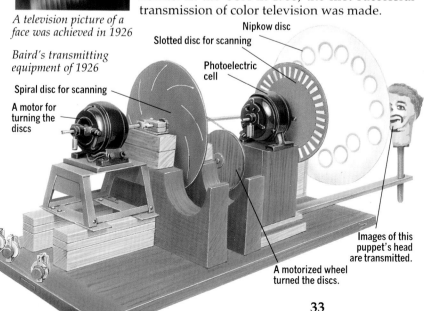

Spiral disc for scanning

A motor for turning the discs

Slotted disc for scanning

Nipkow disc

Photoelectric cell

Images of this puppet's head are transmitted.

A motorized wheel turned the discs.

Hi-tech television

High definition television (HDTV) was first broadcast on June 25, 1990. It was a transmission of the football match between Italy and Uruquay in the 1990 World Cup. HDTV was developed by a group of companies called Eureka 95. Television pictures are made up of lines and tiny dots called pixels. On an ordinary television set there are 625 lines and 120,000 pixels. On a HDTV there are 1,250 lines and 480,000 pixels giving the picture greater detail and clarity.

HDTV produces very realistic images.

The large number of pixels makes the image on an HDTV clear and detailed

HDTV screens can be much larger than normal TV screens.

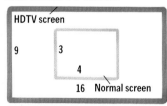

HDTV screen

9   3

4

16   Normal screen

The height/width ratio of a normal TV screen is 3:4, while that of an HDTV screen is 9:16.

HDTV viewing conditions

Range of vision

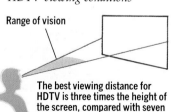

The best viewing distance for HDTV is three times the height of the screen, compared with seven times for normal televisions.

Recording sound

After the invention of the telephone in 1876, many scientists began to research the possibilities of saving or storing sound. Once this had been achieved, inventors continually tried to improve methods of recording sound and playing it back. The machinery has become more and more sophisticated and the sound quality better and better.

A prolific inventor

During his lifetime an American-born inventor named Thomas Edison (1847-1931) registered 1,093 patents. In 1876, he set up the world's first industrial research laboratory, which he called his "invention factory". However, some inventors accused Edison of stealing their ideas.

In 1877, he produced the phonograph, one of his most famous inventions. This machine could record sounds and play them back. At first it was sold as a toy, but before long Edison and other inventors had improved its design so that it could be used to record music.

Edison's phonograph of 1877

A horn focused sound onto a metal diaphragm which touched a steel needle, called a stylus.

Sound made the diaphragm vibrate, causing the stylus to make indentations of different depths in tin foil wrapped around a wax cylinder.

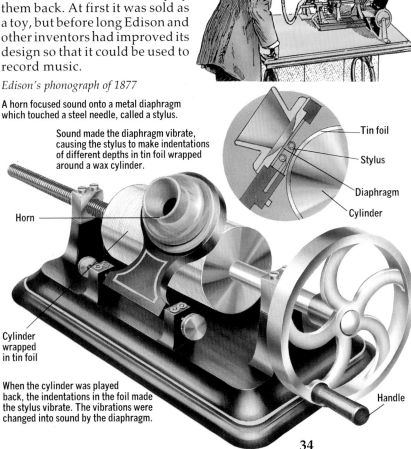

Tin foil
Stylus
Diaphragm
Cylinder

Horn

Cylinder wrapped in tin foil

When the cylinder was played back, the indentations in the foil made the stylus vibrate. The vibrations were changed into sound by the diaphragm.

Handle

The gramophone

Émile Berliner (1851-1929) was a German scientist who emigrated to the USA to seek his fortune. He set up a laboratory where he researched into acoustics (the science of sound) and electricity.

In 1887, he patented a new device which he called the gramophone, after the Greek for "recorded voice". Instead of the cylinders used by Edison, Berliner stored sound in grooves on flat discs made of a substance called shellac (a resin produced by insects). The discs were played back using a needle which vibrated between the walls of the groove on the disc. The recording was played back through a loudspeaker. Berliner's discs produced a much clearer sound than Edison's cylinders.

Horn
Needle
Disc

Berliner's gramophone of 1895

Recording an early Berliner disc

This man is speaking into a mouthpiece and his voice is recorded on a disc.

Mastering

In 1891, Berliner introduced "mastering", a system used to produce many copies of a disc. A glass disc coated with shellac (called a negative) was used to engrave a recording pattern onto flat metal discs (positives). Later, he developed a system in which shellac positives were pressed from a nickel-plated negative. By 1908, Berliner's German factory was producing over six million discs a year. For the first time, people were able to listen at home to music recorded in concert halls.

Mastering a modern vinyl disc

1. Grooves are cut into a master disc made of a very hard plastic called lacquer.

2. The master disc is coated with nickel which is peeled off to be used as a negative.

3. Hot plastic is pressed between two negatives, to produce a positive.

Tape recording

The forerunner of modern tape recorders was designed in 1898, by Valdemar Poulsen (1869-1942), a Dane. He developed a machine called the telegraphone, which converted sound waves into magnetic patterns stored on a wire. To play back the sound, the wire was wound past a magnet. It generated tiny electric pulses which corresponded to the sound originally recorded. These pulses were converted back into sound waves, heard through headphones.

This 1903 Poulsen telegraphone recorded sounds on wire.

The invention of plastic tape turned the tape recorder into a commercial success. It was introduced in 1935 by AEG, a German company. The tape was coated with magnetic particles. It was light and compact, and enabled people to make longer recordings than on discs.

Today, recordings can be made on small audio cassette tapes.

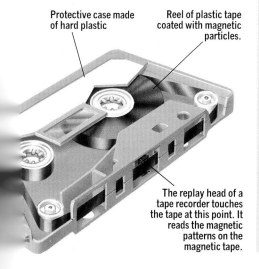

Protective case made of hard plastic

Reel of plastic tape coated with magnetic particles.

The replay head of a tape recorder touches the tape at this point. It reads the magnetic patterns on the magnetic tape.

Compact discs

In 1982, a Dutch company called Philips, and the Japanese firm Sony, introduced the first compact discs. On a compact disc, sound is stored as digital information in tiny pits on the surface. A laser beam scans the pits, and the information is converted into electrical signals and then into vibrations. There is no contact between the laser scanner and the disc, so compact discs do not wear out. They are also unaffected by scratches and dust. A compact disc can store about an hour of music.

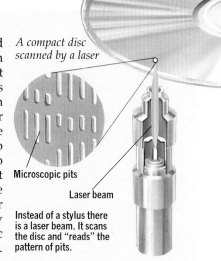

A compact disc scanned by a laser

Microscopic pits

Laser beam

Instead of a stylus there is a laser beam. It scans the disc and "reads" the pattern of pits.

Digital audio tapes

Digital audio tapes (DAT) were introduced in 1987. They are half the size of previous audio cassette tapes, yet they can record two hours of music on each side. Sound is recorded onto these tapes as a numbered code.

Recording sound on to digital audio tapes

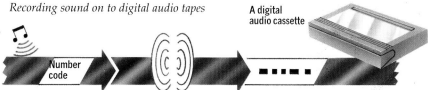

A digital audio cassette

Number code

To record music onto DAT, sound is converted into a code of numbers. Inside a DAT recorder this code is converted into a magnetic pattern.

The magnetic pattern is recorded onto the DAT.

To play back the music on a DAT, this process happens in reverse. The magnetic patterns on the tape are converted into sound signals reproducing the original music.

Movie soundtracks

In 1889, Thomas Edison's assistant Charles Batchelor experimented with combining moving pictures and sound. Over the next 40 years other inventors, many of them associated with the new motion picture industry, developed methods for synchronizing film and speech.

Diagram showing how a film's soundtrack works

1. A stripe along the edge of a movie film carries the soundtrack. The width of this sound stripe varies according to the sound signals produced during the recording.

2. A light is shone through the sound stripe toward a photoelectric cell. The varying width of the stripe varies the amounts of light reaching the photoelectric cell.

3. The photoelectric cell converts the light into sound signals, which are the same as those of the original.

4. The sound signals travel down a cable to the cinema loudspeakers, where they are converted into sound waves.

Lifesavers

Life in the home and at work has always been fraught with dangers. Inventions and technological advances, such as motor cars or aircraft, create new dangers for the people using them. Inventors have had to develop safety devices to compensate for these hazards.

A miner's lamp

Working in mines has always been dangerous. Before the beginning of the 19th century, many miners were killed or injured by explosions when the candles they carried underground ignited pockets of gas. In 1815, an Englishman named Humphry Davy (1778-1829), produced a lamp in which the flame enclosed by fine wire mesh. This stopped the lamp's flame from igniting gas in the air. The number of gas explosions in mines fell dramatically soon after the lamp was introduced.

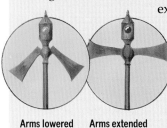

A cutaway of Davy's safety lamp

The wire mesh absorbed the heat of the flame before it could come into contact with the gas in the air.

Wick in oil

Extinguishing fires

In 1816, an English inventor named George Manby, designed a fire extinguisher. It consisted of a metal cylinder containing water. The water was forced out of the cylinder by compressed air.

Alexander Laurent, a Russian inventor, designed the first chemical fire extinguisher in 1905. Foam which smothered flames was pumped by hand out of a metal container.

A modern fire extinguisher uses carbon dioxide gas. When the handle is pressed, a valve opens. This releases the pressure inside, and allows the carbon dioxide to turn into a gas which shoots out of the nozzle.

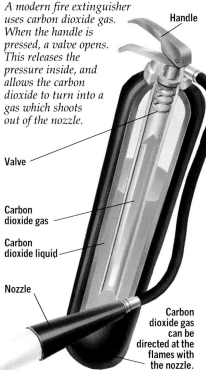

Handle

Valve

Carbon dioxide gas

Carbon dioxide liquid

Nozzle

Carbon dioxide gas can be directed at the flames with the nozzle.

Hidden points

Brooches made of bronze and of a similar design to modern safety pins were used to fasten cloaks in western Europe in the 12th century BC. The modern safety pin itself was designed in 1849, by Walter Hunt of New York.

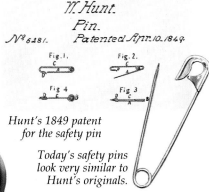

Hunt's 1849 patent for the safety pin

Today's safety pins look very similar to Hunt's originals.

Jumping safely

There is a design for a parachute among the drawings of Leonardo da Vinci (see page 45). However, it was not until 1783 that a parachute was used. A Frenchman named Louis Lenorand used one to jump from a high tower. Many early parachutes looked like umbrellas.

Silk parachutes which fold away were introduced in the USA in about 1880. The first parachute with a ripcord was used in the USA in 1908.

Leonardo da Vinci's design for a parachute

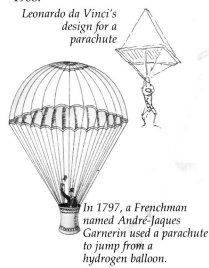

In 1797, a Frenchman named André-Jaques Garnerin used a parachute to jump from a hydrogen balloon.

Green for go

In 1868, a traffic signal arm used to indicate stop and go was first used in London. It had red and green gas lamps for use at night. But the signal was abandoned after an incident in which a gas lamp exploded, killing a policeman.

In 1914, the first electrical traffic light, hand-operated and using red and green lights only, was installed in Cleveland, Ohio. The first automatic traffic lights with red, green and amber lights were installed in London in 1925.

The first traffic signal, installed in London in 1868

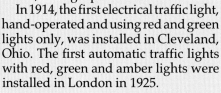

Arms lowered meant "go"

Arms extended meant "stop"

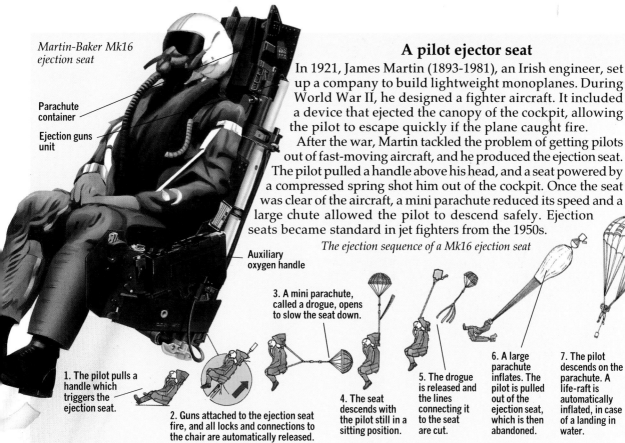

Martin-Baker Mk16 ejection seat

Parachute container

Ejection guns unit

Auxiliary oxygen handle

A pilot ejector seat

In 1921, James Martin (1893-1981), an Irish engineer, set up a company to build lightweight monoplanes. During World War II, he designed a fighter aircraft. It included a device that ejected the canopy of the cockpit, allowing the pilot to escape quickly if the plane caught fire.

After the war, Martin tackled the problem of getting pilots out of fast-moving aircraft, and he produced the ejection seat. The pilot pulled a handle above his head, and a seat powered by a compressed spring shot him out of the cockpit. Once the seat was clear of the aircraft, a mini parachute reduced its speed and a large chute allowed the pilot to descend safely. Ejection seats became standard in jet fighters from the 1950s.

The ejection sequence of a Mk16 ejection seat

3. A mini parachute, called a drogue, opens to slow the seat down.

1. The pilot pulls a handle which triggers the ejection seat.

2. Guns attached to the ejection seat fire, and all locks and connections to the chair are automatically released.

4. The seat descends with the pilot still in a sitting position.

5. The drogue is released and the lines connecting it to the seat are cut.

6. A large parachute inflates. The pilot is pulled out of the ejection seat, which is then abandoned.

7. The pilot descends on the parachute. A life-raft is automatically inflated, in case of a landing in water.

Saved by a cat

An Englishman named Percy Shaw (1890-1976) made a fortune from one simple invention. One foggy night in 1933, he almost drove his car off the edge of a cliff. He was only saved by seeing his headlights reflected in the eyes of a cat sitting at the side of the road. Inspired by this incident, Shaw invented reflecting devices that he called "cat's eyes". They were soon fitted on roads in many countries.

How a cat's eye works

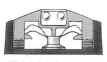

A glass stud is mounted in a rubber case with a metal surround. The mounting is raised above the level of the road.

When a car passes over it, the stud descends into its rubber casing. This reduces obstruction to the car's wheel.

Once the car has passed, the stud rises again and the glass is wiped clean by a rubber pad.

Strapped down for safety

Many inventions have attempted to make people's chances of surviving a car collision greater. In 1903, Gustave Liebau, a Frenchman, patented a design for protective braces, used in cars and aircraft. This formed the basis of the modern seat belt. The Swedish car manufacturer Volvo first fitted seat belts to their cars in 1963.

In 1988, the Japanese car manufacturer Toyota fitted an electrical system in some of its cars that automatically fastens the belt. The following year, Kim Nag-Hyun of South Korea developed a system that, in the event of a collision, automatically releases the belt 30 seconds after impact.

Piston

Explosive charge

Seat belt

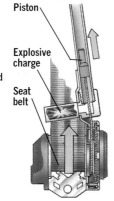

Automatic belt tensioners – On impact, the piston is pushed up by an explosive charge, tightening the belt.

Stages in a head-on collision of a car and a wall

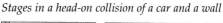

Head-on collisions cause deceleration from running speed to zero in an instant.

As the front of the car crumples it absorbs some of the impact of the collision.

But passengers not wearing seat belts will be thrown forward at high speed.

Stages in the activation of an airbag safety system.

An airbag system contained in the driver's steering wheel is activated on impact.

The airbag inflates to further absorb the energy of sudden deceleration.

When the driver is thrown forward the airbag protects him or her from serious injury.

Medical inventions

Many important inventions have helped doctors to diagnose and treat diseases. Some devices have been developed by doctors themselves, others have been produced as a result of technological advances in other fields which have then been applied to medicine.

Helping nature

Forceps are a surgical instrument used to help in the delivery of babies. They were invented by an English doctor named Peter Chamberlen (d.1631). For many years they remained a well-kept family secret, until Chamberlen's nephew, also named Peter Chamberlen (1601-83), inherited them. His use of forceps made him internationally famous in the field of childbirth.

Chamberlen's original forceps. They were like large pincers, operated by hand.

Ambulances

Dominique Larrey (1766-1842) was a French surgeon who received a gold medal for inventing a curved surgical needle. He is also famous for the invention of the ambulance. In 1792, France was at war with Prussia and Austria. Larrey saw that heavy wagons could not get to the battle front to collect wounded soldiers. He designed a light-weight carriage to transport people to hospitals quickly.

Larrey's ambulance carriage of the 1790s

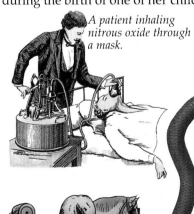

Patients were placed on a thin mattress

Listening to the body

While out walking in Paris in 1816, a French doctor named René Laënnec (1781-1826) saw two children playing. One child held a stick to his ear, while the other child tapped the opposite end with a pin. The sound of the blows was transmitted along the wood. Later, Laënnec rolled up a sheet of paper and tied it with string. When he placed the tube on a patient's chest he could hear a heartbeat. He called his instrument a stethoscope, after the Greek word *stethos* meaning chest.

Try making a stethoscope of your own.

Laënnec's wooden stethoscope

Take a large, rectangular piece of stiff paper or cardboard and roll it into a long tube.

Tie the tube securely with pieces of string or rubber bands to keep it in shape.

Hold one end of the tube to your ear and place the other end against a friend's chest.

Painless operations

An anesthetic is a drug that causes a temporary loss of feeling in a part of the body. Before anesthetics were invented, patients had to be held down by force during painful operations.

The pain-numbing effects of nitrous oxide were first noticed in 1799 by Humphry Davy (1778-1829), an English scientist. In 1846, an American dentist, William Orton, used a powerful anesthetic called ether to perform an operation on a patient's jaw. The following year, a Scottish doctor used a liquid called chloroform to reduce the pain of childbirth. In 1853, chloroform was given to Queen Victoria of England during the birth of one of her children.

A patient inhaling nitrous oxide through a mask.

The "Letheon" ether inhaler was produced in 1847.

Pieces of sponge were soaked in ether.

A mouthpiece was placed over the patient's mouth.

A flexible rubber tube

Ether fumes

Valves in the mouthpiece enabled the patient to breathe in and out.

Injecting beneath the skin

The hypodermic syringe, used to inject drugs into blood vessels or muscles, was invented in 1853 by Frenchman Charles Pravaz.

In 1987, another French doctor, Jean-Louis Brunet, patented a device which is attached to syringes when taking blood samples. The device automatically seals the needle as soon as it is withdrawn from the patient. This reduces the risk of doctors and nurses becoming contaminated by blood infected with dangerous viruses such as AIDS or hepatitis.

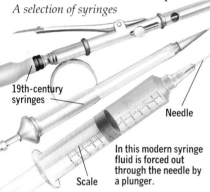

A selection of syringes

19th-century syringes

Needle

In this modern syringe fluid is forced out through the needle by a plunger.

Scale

Monitoring the heart

In 1903, Willem Einthoven (1860-1927) a Dutch doctor, invented the electrocardiograph (ECG) machine. It measures and records the electrical impulses produced by the heart's activity and is used to detect irregularities which can indicate heart disease. In 1924, Einthoven was awarded a Nobel Prize for his invention. An electrocardiograph machine produces a photographic chart of the heart's pulses, which is known as an electrocardiogram.

Einthoven demonstrating equipment which monitored the heartbeat of a dog.

From submarines to babies

By 1918, French scientists led by Pierre Langevin (1872-1946) had developed the sonar (sound navigation and ranging) system. The system sends out beams of sound waves and any object they meet reflects them back. The pattern of reflections forms a picture of the object. Sonar was installed in submarines and ships to detect other vessels. The principle was used in medicine in the 1950s by Ian Donald, a Scottish doctor. He discovered he was able to study the shape of an unborn baby's body and internal organs by passing pulses of sound through its mother's abdomen. This process, called ultrasound scanning, is used to check the health of unborn children.

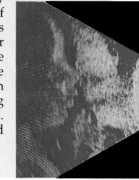

Ultrasound image of a human fetus in the womb

Assisted breathing

In 1929, Philip Drinker, an American engineer, designed a device called a respirator, or iron lung, which helps people with breathing difficulties. It consists of an airtight box enclosing the patient's body from the neck down. Changes of pressure inside the box force air in and out of the lungs.

Early respirator of the 1930s

A 1950s respirator

The patient lies with his or her head outside the airtight box.

Tube to the air pump

A pump created a vacuum inside the airtight box.

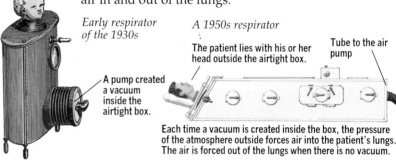

Each time a vacuum is created inside the box, the pressure of the atmosphere outside forces air into the patient's lungs. The air is forced out of the lungs when there is no vacuum.

Surgery using lasers

Doctors often use technology developed for non-medical purposes. Lasers, for example, were first used in industry for drilling, welding and engraving. They are now used in surgical operations to cut through flesh and seal off tiny blood vessels to reduce bleeding. The theory of laser light was suggested in 1958 by Charles Townes (b.1915) and Arthur Schawlow (b.1921), American physicists. The first laser was built in 1960 by Theodore Maiman (b.1927).

How a ruby laser works

A rod of ruby inside a spiral shaped flash lamp.

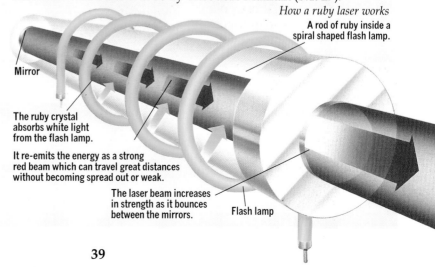

Mirror

The ruby crystal absorbs white light from the flash lamp.

It re-emits the energy as a strong red beam which can travel great distances without becoming spread out or weak.

The laser beam increases in strength as it bounces between the mirrors.

Flash lamp

Weapons and warfare

Weapons are among man's earliest inventions. The first warriors made spears and axes by tying bones and flints to sticks. The Romans used sophisticated mechanical weapons, and by AD1000 the Chinese were making gunpowder for fireworks and sending signals. In the 13th century, Europeans began using gunpowder to fire cannons and hand-held guns.

A 16th-century machine gun. Each barrel had a bullet and was fired by hand.

Today, science and warfare are very closely linked. New and increasingly deadly weapons have been invented by both chemists and physicists.

A fast-firing revolver

Early handguns were very difficult to fire. Before each shot, a gun had to be loaded with gunpowder and pellets, and a fuse lit to ignite it. A more efficient gun was patented in 1836, by Samuel Colt (1814-62) who was born in Connecticut. His gun designs included one called a revolver which could fire six shots before it needed to be reloaded. At first, revolvers were considered very complicated, but later they were extensively used in the American Civil War (1861-65) and by settlers making their way westward across the USA.

This man with two fast-firing revolvers is thought to be Black Jack Ketcham, an outlaw.

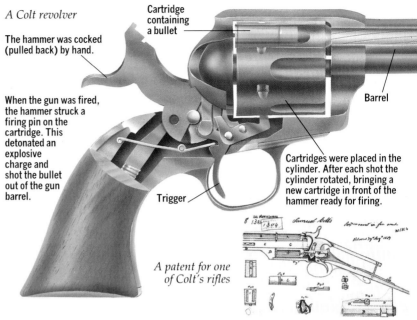

A Colt revolver

The hammer was cocked (pulled back) by hand.

When the gun was fired, the hammer struck a firing pin on the cartridge. This detonated an explosive charge and shot the bullet out of the gun barrel.

Cartridge containing a bullet

Barrel

Cartridges were placed in the cylinder. After each shot the cylinder rotated, bringing a new cartridge in front of the hammer ready for firing.

Trigger

A patent for one of Colt's rifles

A quick killing

Richard Gatling (1818-1903) was an inventor from North Carolina. After the outbreak of the American Civil War in 1861, he designed a gun, called a machine gun, which could be fired rapidly. It had ten barrels arranged as a cylinder around the central shaft. The cylinder was rotated using a hand crank. A cartridge on top of the gun dropped bullets into position for firing. The multiple barrels enabled the gun to be fired many times without overheating. It could fire 350 bullets in a minute.

Gatling's design was improved by Hiram Maxim (1840-1916) who introduced the first fully automatic machine gun in 1884.

A cutaway of a Maxim machine gun

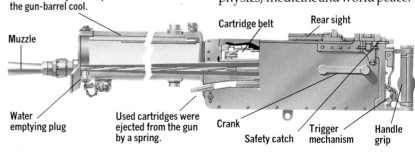

A water-filled jacket kept the gun-barrel cool.

Muzzle

Water emptying plug

Used cartridges were ejected from the gun by a spring.

Cartridge belt

Rear sight

Crank

Safety catch

Trigger mechanism

Handle grip

Dynamite and peace prizes

Alfred Nobel (1833-96), a Swedish chemist, owned a factory that made an explosive called nitroglycerin. When the factory blew up in 1865, killing several people, Nobel began to look for a way to make explosives safer to handle

By mixing nitroglycerin with a chemical called *kieselguhr*, he produced a more stable substance. He sold the mixture in tubes of waxed cardboard and called it "dynamite", after the Greek word *dynamis* meaning power.

Though Nobel made his fortune manufacturing explosives, he was a dedicated pacifist. He left the bulk of his large fortune to fund the Nobel Prizes, awarded annually to people who make major contributions in the fields of literature, chemistry, physics, medicine and world peace.

War rockets

In 1942, a long-range rocket called the V-2 was launched (see page 19). Designed by Wernher von Braun (1912-77), it flew at several times the speed of sound, giving no warning of its approach. It had a range of 320km (200 miles). It had a warhead that weighed about 1.02 tonnes (1 ton) and was packed with explosives.

Today, many missiles are guided to their targets by electronic devices. Some have a range of 9,600km (6,000 miles), and can strike within 30.5m (100ft) of their target.

A V-2 rocket

Nose fuse
Warhead
Fuse conduit
Guidance chamber
Radio control
Nitrogen bottles

This fuel tank contains a mixture of ethyl alcohol and water.

This fuel tank contains liquid oxygen to speed up burning of fuel.

The two fuels are forced by pumps into the combustion chamber. The mixture is then ignited by gunpowder.

The exhaust fumes escape at supersonic speed.

Steerable rudder

Chemical warfare

Fritz Haber (1868-1934) was a German chemist. His early studies involved converting nitrogen (a gas found in air) into ammonia, a substance used in crop fertilizers. He won the Nobel Prize for chemistry in 1918 for this work. But many people objected to the award because Haber had been involved in developing poisonous gases for use in warfare. He produced chlorine gas, which attacks the lining of the nose, throat and lungs. During World War I, both sides used poisonous gases.

Haber also devised a gas mask to protect both civilians and soldiers from harmful gases.

Gas masks were introduced in 1915.

Tight-fitting mask made of cotton pads soaked in chemicals

Connecting pipe

A box containing charcoal and lime-permanganate granules filtered the poisoned air.

Nuclear warfare

By the outbreak of World War II, scientists realized that if the nucleus of an atom was split in two, a huge amount of energy would be released. If this energy was uncontrolled there would be a massive explosion. A bomb based on this principle is called an "atomic bomb".

In 1942, Enrico Fermi (1901-54), an Italian scientist, built a nuclear reactor, in which he produced controlled nuclear energy. The first atomic bomb was developed under the supervision of American physicist Robert Oppenheimer (1904-67). He was in charge of the Los Alamos Science Laboratory, in New Mexico, when the atomic

bomb was tested in 1945. The USA was at war with Japan and later that year they dropped two atomic bombs on the Japanese cities of Hiroshima and Nagasaki, killing many thousands of civilians. When they saw the huge destruction the bomb caused, many scientists spoke out against American plans to build another more powerful bomb, known as the hydrogen bomb or "H" bomb.

Oppenheimer (left) at a bomb testing site

This atomic bomb, called "Fat Boy", was dropped on Nagasaki, Japan.

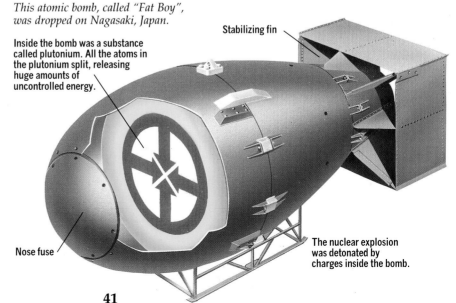

Inside the bomb was a substance called plutonium. All the atoms in the plutonium split, releasing huge amounts of uncontrolled energy.

Stabilizing fin

Nose fuse

The nuclear explosion was detonated by charges inside the bomb.

Calculators and computers

Counting and calculating systems have been needed for as long as people have bought and sold goods. One of the earliest adding machines, the abacus, was invented about 5,000 years ago, in Babylonia (now the area occupied by Iran and Iraq).

A 19th-century engraving of an abacus being used in China

Special numbers

In 1614, John Napier (1550-1617), a Scottish mathematician, invented logarithm tables. The principle of the tables was that every number had an equivalent special number called a logarithm. Logarithms made mathematical division and multiplication quick and easy. For example, to multiply two numbers their logarithms were simply added together. The resulting logarithm was looked up in the tables to find its corresponding number.

An early calculator

Blaise Pascal (1623-62) was a French mathematician. In 1642, he designed an adding machine to help his father, a tax inspector, whose job involved carrying out many complicated calculations.

Pascal's mechanical adding machine

Cogwheels turned dials next to each other in a mechanical gear system

Numbers appeared in these windows.

Dials representing units

Convinced that the machine would make their fortunes, father and son invested a lot of money in it. But their work was opposed both by clerks who feared they would lose their jobs, and by employers who preferred to pay low wages rather than buy Pascal's expensive machine.

Cogs for calculating

Charles Babbage (1792-1871), the son of a rich banker from Devon, England, was a very talented mathematician. He was concerned about errors in Napier's logarithm tables. In 1821, he began to design a "difference engine", a very large and complicated machine, designed to calculate logarithms automatically. But it was difficult to make the machine's parts accurate enough to prevent errors in its calculations.

For about ten years the British government poured money into Charles Babbage's project. But, finally, they lost patience and stopped.

Next, Babbage began to design an "analytical engine", which could carry out many different types of calculation. Working with him was mathematician Ada Lovelace (1815-52). She devised several computer programs for the engine, which were coded on cards with holes punched in them.

Punched program cards

A modern reconstruction of Babbage's analytical engine. It was designed to be driven by steam.

Numbers were stored in columns by wheels which could be put in any of ten positions corresponding to the digits 0 to 9.

Babbage devoted the last 37 years of his life to building the analytical engine. He refined his design again and again, and applied for extra funds to pay for the work. He became increasingly frustrated by what he considered a lack of public recognition and support for his work. In 1871, he died before he had completed the machine. In fact, his engine was well beyond the technology of the time and it is unlikely that it would ever have been finished.

Lady Ada Lovelace became the first computer programmer.

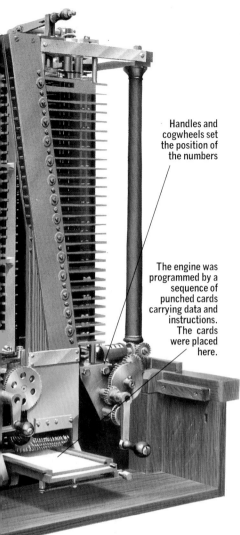

Handles and cogwheels set the position of the numbers

The engine was programmed by a sequence of punched cards carrying data and instructions. The cards were placed here.

Census collection

In the USA during the 19th century, a census of the population was taken every ten years. This became increasingly complicated as the population grew. In 1887, officials were still struggling to compile the results of the 1880 census. A competition was held to find a quicker method of analysing the figures. It was won by Herman Hollerith (1860-1929), an engineer who designed an electric counting machine. Information about each citizen was stored on a card as a series of punched holes. The position of the holes corresponded to particular characteristics, such as age or marital status. The cards were inserted into the machine. Inside, a set of wires was pushed up against them. When a wire passed through a hole, an electric circuit was completed, making a counter advance by one unit. Hollerith's invention sped up methods of processing data so much that the results of the 1890 census were compiled in only six weeks.

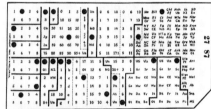

The Hollerith tabulator used to compute the results of the 1890 census.

A card used in the 1900 USA census

Electronic computers

An early electronic computer was ENIAC (Electronic Numerical Integrator and Calculator). It was developed by John Mauchly (1907-80) and John Eckert (b.1919) for the American army. Compared with modern computers it was huge, filling an entire large room. Yet it could perform fewer tasks than a modern desk-top computer.

As technology has advanced, computers have become smaller and smaller,

Eckert (right) holding one of ENIAC's components

yet they are capable of performing an increasing number of tasks.

In 1948, the glass valves, called diodes, used in the first computers (see page 32), were replaced by minute electronic devices called transistors. They were invented by three scientists: John Bardeen (b.1908), Walter Brattain (1902-87) and William Shockley (1910-89), who were jointly awarded the Nobel Prize for physics in 1956. Today, pocket calculators and computers contain tiny electrical circuit boards (called silicon chips) which include thousands of transistors.

Today, computers are used for many tasks, from composing music and creating graphics, to guiding aircraft and milking cows. You can find out more about computers and the tasks they perform on page 22.

A cutaway picture of a pocket calculator

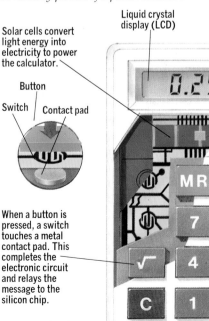

Liquid crystal display (LCD)

Solar cells convert light energy into electricity to power the calculator.

Button

Switch   Contact pad

When a button is pressed, a switch touches a metal contact pad. This completes the electronic circuit and relays the message to the silicon chip.

The power of the imagination

Throughout the centuries, inventors have imagined machines that were beyond the technological capabilities of their time. Other inventors imagined machines which we now know are beyond the realms of possibility. Some of these inventions never went further than the drawing board; others were built, tested and rapidly forgotten.

Wishful thinking

Some of the machines that inventors have believed possible in the past may seem ridiculous to us today. For example, some people believed that it was possible to build a machine which would go on working forever, without an outside power source. This was known as a perpetual motion machine. In 1618, an English doctor named Robert Fludd (1574-1637) designed a perpetual motion watermill. He believed that once the machine was moving it would continue forever. We now know that it is impossible to achieve perpetual motion. The moving parts of a machine rub together and produce friction. This wastes energy and slows the machine down.

Science fiction

Science fiction writers create imaginary worlds, filled with weird inventions. Sometimes the creators believe that in the future, with new materials and greater scientific knowledge, their vision may become reality.

A century before men walked on the Moon, the French author Jules Verne (1828-1905) wrote about space travel. Perhaps writers today, when they describe imaginary worlds are predicting how we will live in the future.

A propeller-driven skating outfit designed by William Heath Robinson

Some writers have made fun of science and invention, by dreaming up machines which could not possibly be built. The writer Jonathan Swift's book *Gulliver's Travels* is full of mock inventions, including a magnetic flying island.

Flights of fancy

In 1867, two English inventors, Edmund Edwards and James Butler, designed an aircraft based on the shape of a paper dart. It was fitted with a rudder for side-to-side control and flaps for up-and-down control. But it was powered by a steam engine and needed a furnace and boiler that would have been so heavy that the machine could never have flown.

A steam-powered aircraft designed by Edwards and Butler

Landing springs

Star wars

Archimedes (287-212 BC) was a mathematician born in Sicily. He invented many very efficient devices. He also tried to design a weapon which used giant mirrors to capture and focus the Sun's rays to destroy enemy ships. We now know that Archimedes' idea would not have worked; but even today scientists sometimes attempt projects which are beyond the capabilities of modern technology. In the 1980s the USA announced plans to build the Strategic Defense Initiative (SDI), known as "Star Wars", which involved a system of satellites used to shoot down enemy missiles with lasers. Some scientists believe the system will never work successfully.

A design for Dr. Fludd's perpetual motion watermill

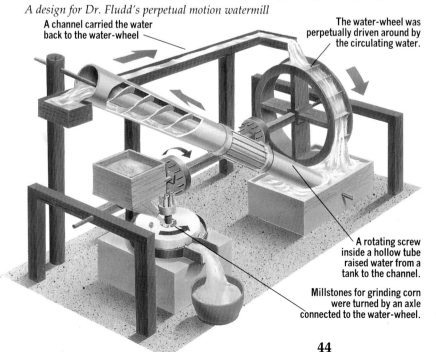

A channel carried the water back to the water-wheel

The water-wheel was perpetually driven around by the circulating water.

A rotating screw inside a hollow tube raised water from a tank to the channel.

Millstones for grinding corn were turned by an axle connected to the water-wheel.

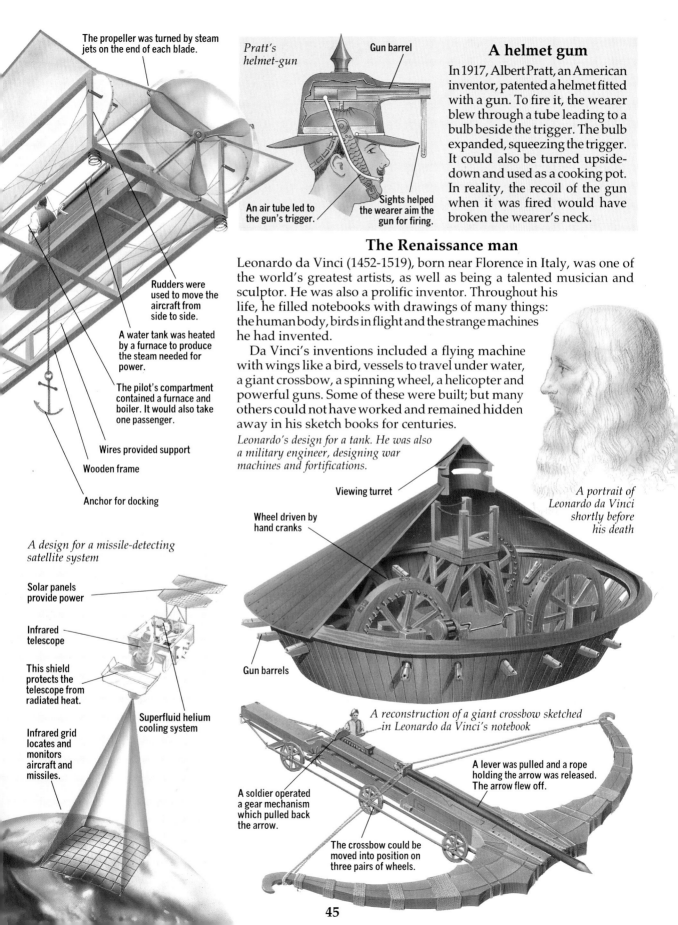

The propeller was turned by steam jets on the end of each blade.

Rudders were used to move the aircraft from side to side.

A water tank was heated by a furnace to produce the steam needed for power.

The pilot's compartment contained a furnace and boiler. It would also take one passenger.

Wires provided support

Wooden frame

Anchor for docking

Pratt's helmet-gun

Gun barrel

An air tube led to the gun's trigger.

Sights helped the wearer aim the gun for firing.

A helmet gum

In 1917, Albert Pratt, an American inventor, patented a helmet fitted with a gun. To fire it, the wearer blew through a tube leading to a bulb beside the trigger. The bulb expanded, squeezing the trigger. It could also be turned upside-down and used as a cooking pot. In reality, the recoil of the gun when it was fired would have broken the wearer's neck.

The Renaissance man

Leonardo da Vinci (1452-1519), born near Florence in Italy, was one of the world's greatest artists, as well as being a talented musician and sculptor. He was also a prolific inventor. Throughout his life, he filled notebooks with drawings of many things: the human body, birds in flight and the strange machines he had invented.

Da Vinci's inventions included a flying machine with wings like a bird, vessels to travel under water, a giant crossbow, a spinning wheel, a helicopter and powerful guns. Some of these were built; but many others could not have worked and remained hidden away in his sketch books for centuries.

Leonardo's design for a tank. He was also a military engineer, designing war machines and fortifications.

Viewing turret

Wheel driven by hand cranks

Gun barrels

A portrait of Leonardo da Vinci shortly before his death

A design for a missile-detecting satellite system

Solar panels provide power

Infrared telescope

This shield protects the telescope from radiated heat.

Superfluid helium cooling system

Infrared grid locates and monitors aircraft and missiles.

A reconstruction of a giant crossbow sketched in Leonardo da Vinci's notebook

A soldier operated a gear mechanism which pulled back the arrow.

The crossbow could be moved into position on three pairs of wheels.

A lever was pulled and a rope holding the arrow was released. The arrow flew off.

Key dates in the history of invention

Dates BC

4241BC The first year in which events can be precisely dated. This is made possible by the introduction of the Egyptian calendar.

c3200BC The Sumerians in Mesopotamia are the first people to use writing and to draw a picture showing a wheel.

c3000BC The Babylonians invent the abacus, the first adding machine.

c1300BC The Syrians develop their own alphabet.

700BC Coins are used in Lydia (Turkey) for buying and selling goods.

287BC The birth of Archimedes, who invents many valuable mechanical devices using screws and levers.

c10BC The Roman architect Vitruvius describes a crane.

Dates AD

999 The first mechanical clock is invented by a monk.

c1000 The Chinese use gunpowder for fireworks and sending signals.

c1045 In China, Pi Cheng invents movable type.

1280 The first pair of glasses is made in Italy.

1450s Johannes Gutenberg's printing presses revolutionize the production of books. This, in turn, speeds up the spread of information about new inventions.

1452 The birth of Leonardo da Vinci, an artist who invents numerous machines.

1569 Mercator a Flemish mapmaker, introduces a new method of drawing maps.

1592 Galileo builds a telescope which magnifies things 30 times.

1614 John Napier, a Scottish mathematician, invents his logarithm tables.

1642 Blaise Pascal designs an adding machine to speed up his father's tax calculations.

1643 Evangelista Torricelli makes a device now known as the mercury barometer for measuring air pressure.

1656 Christian Huygens designs an accurate pendulum clock, based on Galileo's ideas.

1665 The illustrations in Robert Hooke's *Micrographia* reveal the power of new microscopes.

1668 Isaac Newton builds a reflecting telescope.

1698 The first steam engine, built by Thomas Savery, is used for pumping water out of flooded mines.

1733 The flying shuttle, invented by an English weaver, doubles the amount of cloth a person can produce in one day.

1771 Richard Arkwright's water-powered spinning machine produces much stronger cotton thread than was previously possible.

1778 Household sanitation is greatly improved by the introduction of Joseph Bramah's new toilets.

1783 The Marquis de Jouffroy d'Abbans launches the first steamboat.

1783 The Montgolfier brothers successfully fly a hot air balloon.

1797 The value of parachutes is demonstrated by a Frenchman jumping from a hot air balloon.

1801 The *Nautilus*, an early submarine, completes its maiden voyage.

1804 Richard Trevithick builds the first steam locomotive to run on rails.

1814 Friedrich König develops the steam-driven press, which works far more quickly than hand-operated printing machinery.

1815 Humphry Davy invents a miner's lamp, which makes it far safer to work in mines.

1819 Augustus Siebe designs a pressurized diving suit enabling people to dive to greater depths.

1821 Charles Babbage starts work on his difference engine, designed to draw up complicated mathematical tables automatically.

1826 Joseph Niepce, a French physicist, takes the world's first photograph.

1829 George Stephenson wins a competition to design and build the best steam locomotive. He produces a locomotive called the *Rocket*.

1830 The first sewing machine is designed by Thimonnier, a French tailor.

1836 Samuel Colt patents his fast-firing revolver.

1837 Isambard Kingdom Brunel launches the first transatlantic steamship.

1837 Two British inventors named William Cooke and Charles Wheatstone make the first electric telegraph machine.

1839 Louis Daguerre invents daguerreotype photographs, which become very fashionable for portraits.

1843 Samuel Morse designs his famous dot-dash code for use when sending telegraphic messages.

1846 An American dentist uses ether to numb pain during a jaw operation.

1848 The first escalator is opened in New York as a tourist attraction.

1849 The safety pin is invented.

1857 A New York store becomes the first shop to have a safety elevator.

1860 The Belgian Étienne Lenoir builds the first internal combustion engine.

1863 The first underground railway line opens in London.

1868 A newspaper editor, Christopher Sholes, builds the first practical typewriter.

1872 Photographer Eadweard Muybridge takes the first set of sequential photographs.

1876 Alexander Bell sends the first telephone message.

1876 America's most prolific inventor, Thomas Edison, sets up his invention factory.

1877 Edison produces the musical phonograph.

1878 Joseph Swan invents the electric light bulb.

1879 Ernst von Siemens demonstrates the first train to run on electrified tracks.

1881 Émile Berliner patents a gramophone using flat discs.

1884 Hiram Maxim introduces an automatic machine gun.

1885 Physicist Heinrich Hertz demonstrates the existence of electromagnetic waves.

1885 An Austrian chemist named Carl Auer invents a gas mantle, which is easier and safer to use than candles.

1886 Linotype machines enable the text for printed books and newspapers to be produced far more quickly.

1888 George Eastman produces the Kodak no.1 camera and develops customers' films.

1889 Edison's assistant Charles Batchelor experiments with the idea of movie soundtracks.

1890 The Daimler Motor Company starts to manufacture four-wheel, fuel-driven cars.

1890 The American census is rapidly completed with Herman Hollerith's electric counting machine.

1895 In Paris, the Lumière brothers put on a show with ten moving films.

1898 Valdemar Poulson designs the forerunner of the modern tape recorder.

1901 King Camp Gillette patents the disposable safety razor blade.

1902 Italian Guglielmo Marconi transmits a radio message across the English Channel.

1903 The American Wright brothers make the first powered aircraft flight.

1903 Henry Ford introduces mass-production techniques with his new car factory.

1903 Willem Einthoven invents the electrocardiograph machine to record the heart's activity.

1904 John Fleming's glass diodes become an essential part of radio equipment.

1908 Named after its inventor, the Geiger counter is used for detecting and measuring radiation.

1909 The General Electric Company introduces the electric toaster.

1923 Two Swedish engineers design the first refrigerator.

1925 Traffic lights are installed in London.

1926 John Logie Baird successfully transmits the first television image of a human face.

1926 Robert Goddard launches the first liquid fuel rocket.

1928 The American invention "Sellotape" becomes an everyday item.

1929 Philip Drinker invents the iron lung to help sick people breathe.

1933 Two German scientists named Max Kroll and Ernst Ruska introduce the electron microscope.

1933 Inspired by seeing his headlights reflected in an animal's eyes, Percy Shaw invents "cat's eyes" for marking roads.

1935 The German company AEG introduces magnetic plastic tape for recording sound.

1937 People begin to stop using airships after the *Hindenburg* catches fire and passengers are killed.

1938 A Hungarian inventor Lazlo Biro introduces the first ballpoint pen is called a biro.

1938 An American, Chester Carlson, invents the first photocopying machine.

1839 The first helicopter is built by a Russian engineer named Igor Sikorsky.

1942 Wernher von Braun launches the first long-range V-2 rocket.

1942 In Chicago controlled nuclear energy is successfully produced.

1945 An American inventor named Percy Spencer patents his design for the first microwave oven.

1945 The USA drops two atomic bombs on Japanese cities.

1946 ENIAC, America's first electronic computer, is publicly demonstrated.

1947 Edwin Land's Polaroid camera produces black and white photographs in under one minute.

1948 Three American scientists named John Bardeen, Walter Brattain and William Shockley miniaturize electronic circuitry by inventing a device called the transistor and win a Nobel Prize for their work.

1957 The Russian *Sputnik 1* is the first artificial object to orbit the Earth.

1959 The hovercraft, designed by Christopher Cockerell, is publicly demonstrated.

1960 Theodore Maiman builds the world's first laser.

1962 *Telstar* is launched, the first satellite to relay live TV as well as telephone calls.

1977 America launches the Space Shuttle, the world's first reusable spacecraft.

1982 Philips and Sony introduce compact discs.

1987 Digital audio cassettes are introduced.

1990 The first transmission of high definition television.

Index

The picture quiz

This list reveals what the picture or cartoon beside the title of every chapter shows.
p.4   A primitive irrigation machine from Egypt called a shadoof; p.6 An Oriental clock maker; p. 8 Galileo's method of measuring the height of mountains on the moon; p.10 An idea for a steam turbine; p.12 A steam carriage; p.14 A railway policeman of 1844; p.16 Alexander the Great in a glass barrel; p.18 Icarus wearing wings; p.20 A vacuum cleaner operated using a foot pedal; p.22 Carlson's patent drawing for his photocopier; p.24 A toilet designed by John Harington in 1596; p.26 A woodcut of a printer preparing type; p.28 Bell's first telephone; p.30 A 15th century box camera obscura; p.32 A portable radio set; p.34 An illustration showing an Edison phonograph recording a piano (1880); p.36 An early fire fighters' tower; p.38 A clockwork dental drill designed by Harrington; p.40 A hand gun of c.1400; p.42 A machine used to calculate the motion of the Sun and stars; p.44 A design for an aerial cycling machine of 1888

The publishers are grateful to the following organizations for permission to reproduce their material:
CNRI/Science Photo library, p.39; Duckworth, p.44; Fox Talbot Museum, p.1, p.30; The Hulton Deutsch Collection, p.15, p.16, p.19, p.23, p.25, p.32, p.41; Library of Congress, front cover, p.31; Manchester University, p.43; The Mansell Collection, p.12; National Museum of Photography, Film and Television, p.31; Royal Geographical Society, p.7; Syndication International, p.17; Ullstein, front cover.
Elevator compartment illustration, p.24 by Peter Dennis

First published in 1994 by Usborne Publishing Ltd, Usborne House, 83-85 Saffron Hill London EC1N 8RT, England.